DATE DUE

11-19-97		
DEC 1 9 1997		
MAR 1 9 1998		
June 16, 2003		

HIGHSMITH #45115

SUPERVISION
FOR
SUCCESS
IN
GOVERNMENT

Dalton S. Lee

N. Joseph Cayer

SUPERVISION
FOR
SUCCESS
IN
GOVERNMENT

A Practical Guide
for First Line Managers

Jossey-Bass Publishers • San Francisco

For sales outside the United States, contact Maxwell Macmillan International Publishing Group, 866 Third Avenue, New York, New York 10022.

Manufactured in the United States of America. Nearly all Jossey-Bass books and jackets are printed on recycled paper containing at least 10 percent postconsumer waste, and many are printed with either soy- or vegetable-based ink, which emits fewer volatile organic compounds during the printing process than petroleum-based ink.

Library of Congress Cataloging-in-Publication Data

Lee, Dalton S., date.
Supervision for success in government : a practical guide for first line managers / Dalton S. Lee, N. Joseph Cayer. — 1st ed.
 p.   cm. — (The Jossey-Bass public administration series)
Includes bibliographical references and index.
ISBN 1-55542-632-8
 1. Civil service—Personnel management. 2. Supervision of employees. 3. Public administration. I. Cayer, N. Joseph. II. Title. III. Series.
JF1601.L44 1994
350.1'02—dc20   93-43177
                                                                        CIP

FIRST EDITION
HB Printing   10 9 8 7 6 5 4 3 2 1   *Code 9429*

The

Jossey-Bass

Public Administration

Series

Contents

CONTENTS

Preface

This book differs from most books about supervision in several respects. First, it is supported by the experiences of actual supervisors working in public organizations. More than one hundred supervisors were interviewed for this book. They come from a variety of settings: federal, state, and local government; the military; education; not-for-profit organizations; and regulatory, advisory, and service-oriented agencies. Their positions range from top management to front-line supervision, and their experience ranges from a few years to several decades. While they represent the diversity of public sector supervisors, they have several things in common—a commitment to the public they serve, a passion for doing the very best in everything they do, and a willingness to share their experiences so we can all learn how to be more successful supervisors.

Second, the insights offered by these supervisors form the foundation for each chapter. Successful supervisors have a lot of suggestions, methods, tools, procedures, processes, and techniques to share. It was no small task organizing and categorizing this mountain of sage advice to establish a consistent pattern of presentation. In each chapter, typical supervisory problems and issues are identified. Then a variety of strategies for dealing with them are outlined.

Third, this book is specifically about supervision in the public sector. To many authors, supervision is supervision no matter where it is practiced. Consequently, many books on supervision are written for private industry with only occasional references to government and not-for-profit agencies. Certainly there are broad principles of supervision that can be used in both arenas, but we think there are important differences. Supervision in the private sector is evaluated on the basis of only one criterion—how well it supports the bottom line, that is, making a profit. In the public sector, the yardstick for measuring effective supervision is much more complex. Successful supervision in government must recognize not only the economic reality of the organization, but also the political, social, and organizational environment. Often, the natural outcome of our political process is conflicting goals for public organizations and the programs they administer; the focus on accountability sometimes results in an emphasis on bureaucratic approaches rather than motivating the work force; and the struggle for fiscal survival may be at odds with what appears to be the organization's mission. Supervision in the public sector is, in our opinion, a most difficult area of practice, requiring a thoughtful and balanced approach that considers many complex issues such as fairness, equity, and responsiveness.

At the same time that we offer the rich experiences of successful supervisors in the public sector, the reader should be cautioned that we offer no "magic wands." The past decade has presented government with increasingly difficult challenges as political leadership has attempted to accommodate increasingly diverse and complex social values and attitudes in an uncertain economic climate. Some supervisory problems are very intricate and require one to make long-range plans and strategies just to lift one's head above the quagmire. Even though this book cannot solve every problem, it will nevertheless give the reader a sound basis on which to act.

Intended Audience

Supervision for Success in Government was written for those who want to be successful supervisors in public or not-for-profit organizations. It is specifically designed to help the reader deal with thorny issues in supervision. Although this book is aimed at new supervisors and students of supervision, even individuals with experience will find topics not usually included in the typical book on supervision: problems faced in transitioning from worker to supervisor, coping with office politics and political officials, improving public relations, and identifying ethical issues.

Overview of the Contents

Supervision for Success in Government has three parts. Recognizing the individual needs of supervisors, the book is not necessarily designed to be read from cover to cover.

Supervisors who are reading this book may be at different stages in their careers or facing different issues and problems, and they may wish to peruse those parts that apply to their particular situation, then read the rest of the book.

Part One is for the neophyte first line manager. Chapter One identifies common pitfalls that new supervisors face and prepares readers to meet the general challenges of their new role. Chapter Two is designed to help new supervisors deal with the interpersonal aspects of their job transition.

Part Two focuses on key skills and responsibilities of a successful supervisor. Chapter Three demystifies one of the more crucial activities of supervision—decision making. Experienced supervisors comment on the problem-solving model and suggest ways to improve it. Chapter Four discusses leadership and shows how to develop skills to become an effective leader. Since supervisors cannot do the job alone, in Chapter Five the reader learns how to build a winning team. Chapter Six explores different means for influencing the direction of work and suggests several unobtrusive methods for getting the job done. Then, in Chapter Seven, the cornerstone of successful supervision—strategic planning—is examined by veteran supervisors.

Part Three deals with practical problem solving for supervisors. The subject of Chapter Eight is politics—both the internal variety we know as office politics and the external version that emanates from politicians. Chapter Nine advises the aspiring supervisor on how to deal with public and media relations. Seasoned supervisors talk about their experiences and how they have dealt with journalists. Chapter Ten helps the new supervisor prevent and deal with discipline problems. Finally, Chapter Eleven gives the reader a framework for assessing ethical issues.

Acknowledgments

We have many people to thank for helping to make *Supervision for Success in Government* possible.

We are deeply indebted to the many supervisors who came forward and answered our questions in fairly lengthy interviews. Some asked that their responses be treated anonymously because of the nature of their positions. Because their insights and observations were extremely valuable in shaping our understanding of supervision, we have respected that request and have disguised certain details that might reveal their identity.

We are especially grateful to those supervisors who allowed us to use their names. Their personal experiences add immeasurably to our knowledge of successful supervision. In alphabetical order, they are: Barbara A. Baker, Lori Beliveau, Leroy T. Brady, Hattie Bryson, Gregory D. Cantor, Ethel M. Chastain, Gerald Chiles, Daniel Del Castillo, Paul Desrochers, Ron Friedman, Cheryl Fruchter, Mauro Garcia, Larry J. Gardner, Jim Green, Ruth Ann Hageman, Kevin Hardy, Felipe Hernandez, Lee Hultgren, Robert L. Hutchinson, Cleve Jacobs, David Labadie, Carol J. "C. J." Lucke, Charles D. Marshall, William J. McGuigan, Margaret Mudd, Robert A. Nelson, Robin Niklas, Samuel L. Oates, Linda Oravec, Michael Ott, Margaret Owens, J. D. Sandoval,

Marie Schmidt, Bobbie Shaw, Charles Sippial, Rich Snapper, Gary Stephany, Jon Torchia, Tim Vasquez, Janice Weinrick, Reba Wright-Quastler, and Patricia Zamary.

In addition, we sincerely thank the following students who helped collect the data in the pursuit of knowledge: Theo Bautista, Yonas Bayisa, Jacqueline Boco, Jonathan Epps, LaShawn Grant, Scott Hebert, Irene Herrera, Jeff Hunter, Kammie Jackson, Michell Marsh, Cheryl Martinez, Enrique Martinez, Melissa Mathes, Ryland Means, Chris Munroe, Gustavo Reynoso, Jeff Robles, Larry Scularck, Robin Stanko, Perry Tenorio, Raquel Torres, Lonze Townsend, Baldemar Troche, and Bryce Wilson.

A special thanks to the "revision division," Cherylene Schick, for putting this book together.

And finally, we owe our significant others many hours of love in return for their patience, perseverance, and unconditional support during the many months it took to produce this work.

December 1993   Dalton S. Lee
                                   San Diego, California

                                   N. Joseph Cayer
                                   Tempe, Arizona

The Authors

Dalton S. Lee is associate professor of public administration in the School of Public Administration and Urban Studies at San Diego State University, where he teaches management, organization theory, and organizational behavior. He graduated with Great Distinction from the University of California, Berkeley, with an A.B. degree (1968) in psychology and social welfare. He received his M.S.W. degree (1970) from the University of Michigan, Ann Arbor, and his M.P.A. (1983) and D.P.A. (1986) degrees in public administration from Arizona State University.

Lee's many experiences as a supervisor and manager in the public and not-for-profit sector have contributed to his writings in public management. He is the author of *The Basis of Management in Public Organizations* (1990) and has had articles published in *Public Administration Review*,

International Journal of Public Administration, Public Administration Quarterly, Public Productivity Management Review, Review of Public Personnel Administration, and *Journal of Volunteer Administration.*

N. Joseph Cayer has been professor in the School of Public Affairs at Arizona State University since 1982 and director of the school since 1988. He received both his B.A. degree (1964) in political science and his M.P.A. degree (1966) in public administration at the University of Colorado, Boulder, and earned his Ph.D. degree (1972) from the University of Massachusetts in political science.

Cayer's books include *Handbook of Training and Development for the Public Sector* (1993, with M. Van Wart and S. Cook), *Public Personnel Administration in the United States* (2nd ed., 1988), *Managing Human Resources* (1980), *American Public Policy: An Introduction* (4th ed., 1992, with C. Cochran, L. Mayer, and T. R. Carr), and *Public Administration: Social Change and Adaptive Management* (1988, with L.F. Weschler). He has also contributed chapters to various other works and has had numerous articles published in leading public affairs journals. His teaching and research interests lie in public personnel, public labor relations, and general public administration.

Supervisors Whose Names Appear in this Book

Dr. Barbara A. Baker is public administrator, Office of the Public Administrator, County of San Diego. She has over twenty-five years of supervisory experience in her thirty years of work experience.

Lori Beliveau is recreation services manager, City of El Cajon, California.

Dr. Leroy T. Brady is director of human resources for the City of San Diego Police Department.

Hattie Bryson is office manager in the Student Outreach Services Program at San Diego State University. She has been a supervisor for over a third of her twenty-one years in public service.

Gregory D. Cantor is a sergeant in the La Mesa, California Police Department. He is currently a training manager.

Ethel M. Chastain is director of human resources, County of San Diego. She has been a supervisor for twenty-three years and worked in the public sector for twenty-four years.

Gerald Chiles is supervising personnel analyst for the City of San Diego. He has over four years of supervisory experience and has worked in the public sector for over a decade.

Daniel Del Castillo is a personnel management specialist in the Personnel Services Department at San Diego State University. He has been a supervisor for ten years.

Paul Desrochers is assistant vice president of operations for Centre City Development Corporation in San Diego.

Ron Friedman is a principal planner in the City of San Diego Planning Department.

Cheryl Fruchter is principal management analyst in the City of Chula Vista, California.

Mauro Garcia is a human resource development specialist in the City of San Diego Organizational Development Program.

Larry J. Gardner is labor relations manager, City of San Diego.

Jim Green is a highway mechanic supervisor for the California Department of Transportation.

Ruth Ann Hageman is director of the Citizens' Assistance Office, City of San Diego.

Kevin M. Hardy is a principal management assistant for the Police and Fire Departments of the City of Chula Vista, California. He has three years' supervisory experience.

Felipe Hernandez is adjutant, Headquarters and Service Battalion, United States Marine Corps Depot, San Diego. He has been a supervisor in the public sector for over thirteen years.

Lee Hultgren is director of transportation at the San Diego Association of Governments (SANDAG). She has over eighteen years of supervisory experience.

Robert L. Hutchinson has been an administrative assistant in the Department of Health Services, County of San Diego, after serving in the Air Force for many years.

Cleve Jacobs is a personnel analyst in the Personnel Department in Chula Vista, California. He has been a supervisor for over five years.

David Labadie is a training supervisor at the San Diego County Juvenile Hall. He has been a supervisor for two years and been a public employee for over seventeen years.

Carol J. "C.J." Lucke is an associate administrative analyst in the Waste Management Department of the City of San Diego. She has been a supervisor for a year.

Charles D. Marshall is human resource officer and captain in the City of San Diego Fire Department. Half of his twenty-year career has been in a supervisory capacity.

Margaret Mudd has been a supervising probation officer for the County of San Diego Probation Department for over two years.

Robert A. Nelson is interim public works director for the City of Encinitas, California. He has been a supervisor for over three decades.

Robin Niklas is supervisor of mail delivery in the La Jolla, California Post Office and has twenty-one years of public sector experience.

Samuel L. Oates is an assistant fire marshal in the City of San Diego Fire Department.

Linda L. Oravec is executive director of ADAPT Programs, Inc. She is a former city councilperson.

Michael Ott is assistant executive director, San Diego Local Agency Formation Commission (LAFCO). He has three years of supervisory experience.

Margaret Owens is a secretary in the Department of Land Use and Planning, County of San Diego.

J. D. Sandoval is planning and community development director for the City of Del Mar, California. He has a decade of supervisory experience.

Marie Schmidt is a principal in the San Ramon Valley Unified School District in Danville, California. She has over nine years of supervisory experience and has worked twenty-two years in the public sector.

Bobbie Shaw is an administrative assistant in the Equal Opportunity Program/Ethnic Affairs at San Diego State University. She has spent twelve of her twenty-three years of public sector experience as a supervisor.

Charles Sippial is director of the San Diego State University physical plant. He has over a quarter century of supervisory experience in the public sector.

Rich Snapper is director of personnel, City of San Diego.

Gary Stephany is deputy director, Department of Health Services, County of San Diego. He has acted in a supervisory capacity for almost two decades and has worked in the public sector for thirty years.

Jon Torchia is a captain in the La Mesa, California Fire Department. He has nine years of public sector experience and four years of experience as a supervisor.

Tim Vasquez is chief of the Environmental Analysis Branch of CALTRANS. He has over thirty-five years of work experience and twenty-six years of experience as a supervisor.

Janice Weinrick is redevelopment director in the City of La Mesa, California Redevelopment Agency.

Reba Wright-Quastler is director of planning in the City of Poway, California.

Patricia Zamary is personnel services manager in the Department of Human Resources, San Diego County where she has over ten years of supervisory experience. She has worked in the public sector for over a quarter century.

SUPERVISION
FOR
SUCCESS
IN
GOVERNMENT

Part One

ON BECOMING
A FIRST LINE
MANAGER

1

Now What Do I Do? Understanding the Supervisor's Role

What all first-time supervisors seem to have in common is that they worked very hard to get promoted. Most were more productive and efficient than the average worker. For many a commitment to excellence did not have to be taught, it was already a deeply ingrained value. Why, then, do we hear so many horror stories about supervisors who cannot lead, who cannot delegate, who cannot give credit where credit is due, and who cannot take responsibility for their own actions?

Part of the answer lies in the distinction that must be made between being an exceptional worker with the potential to become a supervisor and being an actual supervisor with considerable supervisory skills. Exceptional workers are able to discipline themselves, but exceptional supervisors must impart that same discipline to others. It is easier said than done. It is one thing to work hard to make oneself happy but quite another to create an entire work environment that other workers will find satisfying and rewarding.

Indeed, supervision is a new skill that needs to be mastered, but gaining the needed experience and training is not easy. Some organizations provide little or no supervisory training. When training is available, it may come months after a person has assumed the new position, too late to be of much use.

Because it is not uncommon for productive workers to be promoted to supervisory positions without an adequate understanding of the supervisory role, we interviewed over a hundred public sector supervisors to find out what they did to make the transition successfully. Their responses fell into two broad categories: assuming the role of the supervisor and convincing others that they could do the job. In this chapter, we explore several key concepts in supervision that every new supervisor should know. In Chapter Two, we deal with several specific techniques for starting off on the right foot. By sharing their experiences, these supervisors make it possible for new supervisors to recognize and deal with many of the common problems encountered in the transition to becoming a successful supervisor.

What Is Supervision?

An important place to begin is by defining supervision. A literal translation of the term is to "oversee" the work of others. This conceptualization of supervision has its origins in ancient times, when masters oversaw the activities of slaves and directed their work. By the Middle Ages, slavery had been replaced by indentured servitude, but because the tedium of work was considered just retribution for leading a sinner's life, supervision had merely traded a physical whip for an economic one. Although there may be some current-day supervisors who take great pleasure in overseeing their workers, the image of a boss standing over workers with a whip (or paycheck) in one hand and pointing an accusatory finger with the other hardly evokes a romantic image of supervision, much less an effective one.

This image of a hard, authoritarian supervisor has no place in today's workplace. Like much of our society, supervision has, thank goodness, evolved. On the brink of the Industrial Revolution, the Protestant Reformation led to improved supervision in America as workers attempted to perfect their productivity for the divine glory of God. To waste time and resources was considered a moral transgression and an abrogation of social duty and responsibility. Clearly, supervisors had an impact on production, and it only seemed reasonable to improve on that impact. So what may have started out as trial and error, void of theory, and inconsistent in practice has become a sophisticated field of study with a shared body of knowledge, common concepts and terminology, and generally accepted principles.

Obviously, supervision still includes directing the work of others, but today we understand it to be a much more complicated process than giving one-way orders. We now

5

know that workers want to contribute to worthwhile purposes they value rather than be handed someone else's goals and objectives to follow. They want to use their creativity to do the best job possible instead of being told what to do, when to do it, and how to do it.

That leads us to a better definition of supervision, one that was shared by the supervisors we interviewed: working through others to accomplish organizational goals. Several points about this definition distinguish it from simply *directing* the work of others.

First, the supervisor is not doing the work, but is working through others. A common error of new supervisors is to continue as if they were still workers doing the work themselves. What needs to be kept in mind is that a supervisor's tools are no longer his or her own hands, but the hands of others.

Second, to work through others requires the supervisor to recognize the needs of others. Because new supervisors were efficient and effective workers, they sometimes think that what worked for them will work for others as well, and they impose solutions where none are needed. What they forget is that it is not just other people's hands doing the work, but their hearts and minds as well. Treating workers as though they cannot think for themselves does little to create commitment and loyalty or reinforce the idea that they are working on important projects.

Third, the purpose of work is not allegiance to the supervisor's personal goals, but to a higher set of goals that transcend the organization. Loyalty should be not to a person, but to the organization's mission and values. In a way, supervision involves identifying and aligning the worker's personal values and needs with the organization's.

As a result, supervision is much less the traditional process of directing the work of others as it is coaching, facilitating, discovering hidden potential, removing barriers, providing resources, and reinforcing existing skills and attitudes.

New Duties and Responsibilities

New supervisors are faced with many questions. One public works supervisor we asked summed it up this way: "When you first start, there is a lot of worry. Is the job going to get done? Is it going to get done right? How much confidence can you place in your people? Are they going to get the job done for you?"

Knowing the intricacies of the worker's job—having technical expertise—is the reason most are promoted to supervisor. That knowledge will serve well in answering technical questions from workers. However, there is more to supervision than addressing technical issues, as the above questions demonstrate. Three comments by veteran supervisors further illustrate the point.

"There is a significant difference between being a competent technician and being a competent manager," says a labor relations manager. "Technical expertise is, in many cases, much more cut and dried. In terms of managerial issues, there are a lot more gray areas for which there may or may not be a right or wrong answer."

"One of the big stresses is that you are changing from working with peers to being responsible for their productivity," says Charles Marshall, a fire department captain. "It is a change in relationship: you are now responsible for their evaluation and the direction given to them. One of the additional adjustments that you have is that you are changing from carrying out policy to directing policy as it comes down."

A supervisor for almost a quarter century put it this way: "Most new supervisors have only been responsible for themselves or a piece of machinery prior to this point. Now they are in the business of training and motivating human beings, the most complex form of life known."

What these supervisors are talking about are the three areas of expertise required to be a successful supervisor: technical, conceptual, and human.

Technical Expertise

Technical expertise involves an understanding of, as well as a proficiency in, a specific type of activity—analyzing a budget, writing a job description, processing a planning permit, or evaluating a client's eligibility for services. It is a specialized knowledge of procedures, processes, and methods.

Having this competence is important to frontline supervisors, because they must teach others how to do the job, answer questions from subordinates, and know if workers are doing what is expected of them. More important, workers tend to respect those supervisors who know what needs to be done.

However, there may be problems with relying too heavily on technical expertise as the basis for supervision. As several seasoned supervisors were quick to point out, new supervisors have to learn to let go of the old job they were doing. "Too often, supervisors who have been 'doers' most of their lives have a difficult time detaching themselves from the 'doer' role," says one supervisor. They continue to do the technical work instead of supervising the work of others.

A planning supervisor recounts an instance of the universal horror story of the supervisor who would not let go. "The supervisor who edited everyone's work created a self-fulfilling prophecy," she tells us. Instead of working through others, he and his workers ended up doing the same work. As a result, "the workers stopped caring about their work. They produced poor quality work and he received a less polished product." To make matters worse, "some would resubmit the original unedited copy and he would approve it anyway or make the same corrections and send it back. He micromanaged—creating a less productive group."

What can be done about this situation? Tim Vasquez, who works for a state transportation department, offers some sage advice. "Don't take the old job with you. As a former engineering supervisor, I use the phrase: 'Don't take the drafting table into the office.'"

If having too much expertise can be a problem, so too can not having enough. "A personal experience of mine is a good example," Vasquez explains. "When I changed departments and became an assistant project engineer, I was in charge of an area for which I did not know the technical aspects. However, I told the others how to do the job my way, not letting them do it themselves. A sort of mutiny towards me evolved. Soon, nothing got done and

9

my supervisor had to have everyone sit down and review each other's duties. Moral of the story: Don't tell people how to do their job, especially if you don't know how yourself!"

This is the point made in the management classic *Modern Organizations* (Thompson, 1961). Some of the tension that is occasionally felt between worker and supervisor is the result of the worker being so specialized that the supervisor can no longer keep up. Consequently, the supervisor has difficulty overseeing the duties of the specialist. If supervisors attempt to use technical expertise (which they do not really have any longer) as a basis for legitimizing their authority over workers, the workers are likely to rebel, as the Vasquez situation proves.

One supervisor suggests the honest approach: "The transition can be eased by telling the workers [about] your unfamiliarity of the area, but [that] you sincerely intend to learn about all its inner workings and about its workers. I've found that by being up-front and honest with subordinates, you gain better respect and cooperation. If you charge in there like some kind of know-it-all, you'll be met by resistance or challenges from the workers."

Does lack of technical knowledge mean that supervisors have lost respect in the eyes of workers? Probably not, because, as we shall see, the basis of supervision does not rest on technical knowledge alone.

Conceptual Expertise

Understanding a unit's mission requires some ability to think in the abstract, and grasping the "big picture" is the essence of conceptual expertise. Locked into habits that proved useful for survival as workers, most new supervisors have a tendency to think in the short term. By focusing on day-to-day activities, supervisors end up being reactive—behind the crisis instead of in front of it, so to speak. True, it is difficult to predict when a specific crisis will occur, but crises seem to frequent the public sector with such regularity—like hurricanes, tornados, and earthquakes—that it seems entirely possible to be prepared to a certain degree.

Conceptual expertise is the ability to think proactively, to be strategic, to diagnose and analyze, to identify cause-and-effect relationships, and to understand how different parts of the organization fit together.

One way to think broadly about the supervisory job is to look at all the activities that a supervisor must perform to have a productive work unit. One handy way to do this is by remembering POSDCORB, an acronym invented by Gulick and Urwick (1937) which represents all of the functions that a public sector supervisor is engaged in: **P**lanning, **O**rganizing, **S**taffing, **D**irecting, **CO**ntrolling, **R**eporting, and **B**udgeting.

Planning involves determining the goals of the work unit, deciding how the goals will be achieved, designing a course of action, and establishing policies and procedures to guide activities. Planning should also include identifying potential barriers and roadblocks as well as strategies for dealing with them. While planning is the most important POSDCORB function, it is probably the most neglected. Most supervisors do too little planning, often

11

arguing that they are forced to focus on flare-ups of interpersonal conflicts within the organization. The danger here, of course, is that supervisors will not know where the unit is going, whether it is making progress toward that goal, or when the mission has been accomplished. (There is more about planning in Chapter Seven.)

Organizing is the initial step in implementing the plan. This step includes assigning tasks to people, setting up work schedules, grouping activities to coordinate effort, and clarifying the lines of authority as well as individual responsibilities. It involves matching available resources with stated objectives and coordinating activities so that the goals can be reached efficiently and effectively.

Staffing pertains to recruiting and selecting people to fill jobs, orienting and training them, and evaluating performance. Although workers assigned to new duties may be highly qualified, they usually need additional instruction on pertinent organizational policies and procedures. They also need to be informed about formal and informal expectations, consequences for performance discrepancies, and the benefits of meeting or exceeding performance standards.

The directing function includes guiding and influencing the work of others, as well as communicating, creating motivation, and handling the expected people problems that emerge in activity involving interaction with others. This is where considerable leadership ability is required. Successful directing means being engaged in general supervision rather than constant, direct supervision. General supervision acknowledges individual differences in motivation and ability by focusing on the accomplishment of goals rather than on the adherence to a specific process at the expense of goal attainment. Direct supervision, as mentioned before, often leads to "micromanaging," which subordinates the worker's specialist knowledge to the supervisor's—regardless of the supervisor's skill. Speaking out against direct supervision, one supervisor says, "Let workers redo their own work until it meets the standards. Don't try to fill somebody else's shoes. Employees can learn from their mistakes. One stops growth when one combats change." "Don't do the job for them," reiterates Vasquez. "Give guidelines and suggestions and let them do it wrong if needed." That is the essence of general supervision.

Supervisors also engage in controlling—that is, collecting information about progress toward goals, comparing the findings to the plans, and taking corrective actions when necessary. It is the process of measuring progress toward stated goals and objectives. The controlling function should not be confused with assuming a dictatorial style with workers.

As information is gathered, public sector supervisors are responsible for reporting findings to superiors and, if required, to the public. The reporting function includes written and oral reports to legislative committees, executive management, other departments, unit workers, and constituents. Reporting is one part of being accountable for those things one is responsible for.

Finally, supervisors are engaged in budgeting—the formulation, acquisition, and allocation of limited resources to achieve the organization's goals. Although budgeting is mentioned last, it links us back to the planning function. Because public sector work is often characterized by limited resources—not enough staff, time, money, materials— each new program or project should begin with a planning phase, followed by organizing, staffing, directing, controlling, reporting, and budgeting. After the budgeting phase, it is time again to reexamine plans, organization structure, staffing patterns, and the rest of POSDCORB. By cycling through these functions on an ongoing basis, it is possible to refine needed changes and simultaneously be prepared for changing conditions. When things have not changed significantly, that does not mean planning stops. Planning continues in order to anticipate and predict the disequilibrium that so often disrupts the status quo in the public sector. By taking the time to set up a POSD-CORB system, new supervisors are beginning to think strategically.

Human Expertise

Since supervisors do not do the work themselves, they must have good interpersonal skills to (1) communicate with others about the quality and quantity of work that must be accomplished; (2) motivate workers to produce at a consistent and high level regardless of the economic, political, and personal circumstances; and, most important, (3) build cooperative relationships among individuals and groups. Unfortunately, expertise in human behavior often seems to be in short supply. As the personnel director of a large company says, "New supervisors come up through the rank and file and go from dealing with technical problems to people problems. The majority are good at doing the technical duties, but need improvement in interpersonal communication and general people skills."

Supervisors must be able to relate to their people in as many ways as their people see them. According to Leroy Brady, a human resources director, "New supervisors must be many things: a director of human resources, a counselor, a motivator, a person who makes suggestions, a father or mother to some, and just a coordinator to others. They are going to be many types of personalities all rolled into one."

Mintzberg (1973) has identified at least ten roles that supervisors perform. He breaks them down into three categories: interpersonal, informational, and decisional. The interpersonal aspects of supervision require that the supervisor at times be a leader, a liaison, and a figurehead. As a leader, the supervisor motivates workers to produce. The role activities range from hiring and firing to directing work activity and offering incentives for performance. In the liaison role, the supervisor coordinates activities between individual workers, among groups of workers in the workplace, and with outside groups as well. The figurehead role involves activities that are primarily symbolic and ceremonial. Giving a tour of the organization, handing out awards, and taking visiting dignitaries to dinner are examples of this role.

Supervisors are also involved in the collection and distribution of information. Mintzberg identifies three distinct informational roles: monitor, disseminator, and spokesperson. The monitor role is concerned primarily with collecting information that is of value. Measures of productivity in the form of monthly activity sheets and computer printouts may be used to monitor internal activities. Supervisors may also read professional journals, attend meetings, and talk with political figures to understand the external environment. When supervisors pass this information on to superiors and subordinates, they are performing the disseminator role. When supervisors make a formal speech or presentation, they are acting as the spokesperson. Needless to say, what information is gathered, to whom it is disseminated, and how it is presented can dramatically influence the way work is perceived.

Finally, Mintzberg identifies four decisional roles: entrepreneur, disturbance handler, negotiator, and resource allocator. In the entrepreneurial role, supervisors initiate change to improve the organization's performance. As disturbance handlers, supervisors resolve conflict so that it does not interfere with organizational progress. Supervisors may serve as negotiators, to facilitate agreement and consensus. In the role of resource allocator, supervisors decide what workers and units could benefit by receiving additional money, materials, time, and manpower.

Ruth Ann Hageman, director of constituent services in a large city, sees it as a challenge. "Motivating people to be excited about their jobs and to perform at their maximum potential is not easy. In the public sector, where there is a dearth of funds compared to the services that need to be performed, it is important that people perform in an extraordinary way. It is kind of the opposite of the usual stereotype of public officials—people who are lazy, or do as little as possible. We have to have people who put out 100 or 110 percent in terms of effort and hours all of the time, whether they are sick or not, compensated or not. So the challenge is to help people love what they are doing, to see the big picture."

Her way of meeting the challenge is simple and makes sense: involve workers in "defining and articulating the mission for the program, whatever it is." The reason that approach works is that there is something onerous about being forced to work on a project when we have little to say about the worthiness of a particular service being rendered. More often than not, we would much rather voluntarily offer our work effort, especially if we can feel committed to the purpose. Even if there is disagreement, as long as we have the opportunity to express our concerns, we can still work on the project.

Agreeing on a Common Purpose

Reaching an agreement about what the mission is and how it should be addressed is not an easy process. Several supervisors mentioned that there was pressure from both upper management and other supervisors to conform to the traditional management style, characterized by one supervisor as "This is the way it is done; this is the way it is going to be done; and there will be no changes."

"They allow little input and very few new ideas to come in," says another. "They use old ideas. That style does not work."

"I thought what I needed to do was to impress my superiors with the kind of supervisor I could be," says a third. "I came in and kicked butt, took names, and found out very quickly that's not the way to go."

Even if one is aware of the traditional management trap, there is still considerable external pressure from both superiors and subordinates to demonstrate that one can influence the quality and quantity of the unit's output. To compound things further, there is often an equally strong internal pressure caused by new supervisors wanting to make changes and improvements once they are finally in a position to make a difference.

However, veteran supervisors caution the novice to resist the urge to make too many changes. It is not because the changes are not needed from a technical and conceptual point of view, but because we are dealing with human beings. To be an effective supervisor requires establishing a workable relationship with workers before anything else can happen. As one supervisor puts it, "In order for new supervisors to prepare themselves to be more effective, they must learn how to treat individuals as individuals and not as subordinates."

Experienced supervisors have several other suggestions for getting along—take your time, reach a consensus, be appreciative, and be honest.

Take Your Time

Collectively, the supervisors we interviewed seemed to agree that there should be no drastic changes when a new person takes over the supervision of a unit. "Don't come in with all these dreams and bulldozer ideas," says a seasoned supervisor. "Just take it one day at a time."

"Supervisors must not make drastic changes. Let the employees adjust to the new period," says Barbara Baker, a public administrator. If you think about it, there has been plenty of change already. The old supervisor's leaving was a change; the new one's arrival on the scene was a change. Routines and habits have been altered. The power in personal, professional, and hierarchical relationships has shifted.

Rushing through changes without examining existing group dynamics may give the impression that the new supervisor is too aggressive. If workers perceive the new supervisor as overly aggressive, one Drug Enforcement Administration supervisor warns "there is a chance you will alienate your employees. And it will take a great deal of time to overcome that initial impression." We know from our own personal experiences how lasting and indelible an incorrect first impression can be.

Brady's advice was to pace oneself like a runner—start slowly and build up energy, wind, and speed. Whether promoted from within or hired from the outside, he believes new supervisors must still "gain an understanding of what employees do. One must gain respect, understanding, and loyalty from workers." Although it may seem silly at first for a supervisor to ask workers about their jobs when the supervisor is supposed to know what they are doing, the suggestion makes a lot of sense given that everyone sees things a little bit differently. For example, one employee may have liked interviewing candidates for a job because coming up with interview questions required creative thinking, but someone else may like the process because of the interpersonal interaction, and someone else

19

may not even like it at all—it may just be a way of earning a paycheck.

It is important to appreciate the time, effort, and talent involved in your work unit, one supervisor points out, because it can help you deal with individuals on a much more personal and understandable basis. One middle manager tells us he tries to ensure that this happens with his new supervisors. "When I bring in new supervisors, I let them have two or three weeks in which they do nothing but talk to the people that they are supervising, go out with them, be with them, listen to their needs. That gives you a pretty good feel about what's happening, what the needs are, and the sensitivities of the job. It is a very effective way to start out in a new supervisory position."

To sum up, as another supervisor puts it, "To be effective you must always give yourself time to consider all possibilities and to earn the respect of your people. You must be compassionate to their needs. In return, if you treat them right, they will do the same for you." After all, someone else reminds us, "Treat them the way you always wanted to be treated. Don't forget, you once were a worker too!"

Reach a Consensus

Building a consensus with staff assumes that there is a solid foundation of mutual respect and understanding underlying the relationship. Supervision is a two-way street. Yes, supervisors have the power to tell people what to do, and yes, even the power to order them to redirect their efforts in ways that the supervisor believes are best for the organization. But keep in mind, supervisors do not have the power to demand respect.

An elementary school principal tells a story about how subtle the process is. A new principal who had not bothered to study the existing routines and cultural norms, she recalls, "went into the lunchroom and chose an empty seat at a table with other faculty members in the hopes of fitting in. However, everyone slowly got up and left, leaving him alone. What had happened was he sat in 'Mrs. Jones's chair' and the staff felt he didn't respect their routine."

While supervisors have the ability to influence some of the social interactions in the work unit, they are not in control of them by any means. "An older manager used to get mid-managers in fights against each other," one supervisor shudders to think. "He told them to report against each other. I guess he figured that they wouldn't organize against him that way. He played 'gotcha games' to gain power and control." Try as he would to control the interactions of his subordinates, it caught up with him in the end. He was later reprimanded and banned from ever working in public service.

Experienced supervisors tell us that successful supervision has less to do with exercising one's power over subordinates and more to do with empowering them to pursue excellence. To do that requires that worker and supervisor build a shared vision with common goals to work toward.

Cheryl Fruchter, a management analyst, puts it eloquently:

Being a supervisor is helping your employees get *their* jobs done because that will in turn get *your* job done. You should make sure that they have a proper en-

21

vironment to do their job. Listen carefully to what they have to say. Try not to tell them exactly how to do the work. Just because you used to do it a certain way doesn't mean that they have to do it precisely the same way you did. You should jointly set the goals you're trying to meet and what quality you'd like the work to be. Talk to them frequently—especially to make sure that you all are on the same wavelength and have the same concept of what doing the job correctly is. And give them a lot of feedback.

Fruchter gives an example of how she would achieve consensus. "Very often if you're supervising clerical staff, the majority of their work is helping other people. So find out what expectations those people have, what expectations the clerks have, and fit them together."

Other supervisors offer their advice on this topic. Make sure your own supervisor has clearly defined the goals and your role vis-à-vis those goals, suggests Hattie Bryson, an office manager. "I would advise them to look at the entire picture when dealing with any situation and not just one part of the picture." Along those same lines, a supervisor of two years says, "If you don't understand your boss's goals or your subordinates' goals, you probably are not going to get the cooperation needed." According to one supervisor of six years, that may mean asking about workers' career plans to see where they are going.

As in all human affairs, people are not always going to agree, but one supervisor of two years recommends, "If you can't empathize with them, you need to treat them as colleagues and not as subordinates." That means lots of communication—sit down with workers, individually and as a group, and make sure that each understands the other. Be a good listener. Allow them to express their feelings about what could be changed and what needs improvement. It is also important to ask them about what they do *not* want to change.

C. J. Lucke, a waste management specialist, offers similar advice: "On a daily basis, try to find out what is going on—even if it's only for five minutes. For example, meeting someone in the hallway and getting an update on events. Whenever you have a free minute, just drop in."

When expectations have been agreed on, it is then possible to elaborate on goals and objectives for the unit. Says Kevin Hardy, a principal management assistant, "Once you've done that, develop your staff and its responsibilities in a way that directly will achieve that set of objectives." If possible, Baker advocates, try to solve a group problem to enhance group unity.

Be Appreciative

Another important element for building a strong relationship with workers is to give credit where credit is due. "You are now the boss," says a supervisor for a utility company, "but you are not a leader unless you have followers. Give credit to the workers for work they have done." Appreciating them, their work, and their daily contributions is important. It makes workers feel not only that they are part of the team, but also that worker and supervisor share a common purpose.

Unfortunately, many supervisors take their workers for granted. By that we do not mean only those supervisors who always seem to forget to say hello, good-bye, thank you, and please, but also those who engage in seemingly benign neglect. It is not uncommon to hear some supervisors say that there is no need to pay special attention to workers who, for example, come to work on time every day. Their excuse is that this is what is expected—this is what they are paid for.

What such supervisors seem to think is that the supervisor's job is only to recognize performance that exceeds standards, the rationale being to motivate workers to strive harder. Yet, by not paying attention to those workers who consistently meet standards, the end result is that the majority of workers are ignored. If supervision is like a marriage, how long will the relationship last if one partner continually ignores the daily contributions of the other?

Build Integrity

"This is a hypothetical situation," says Gregory Cantor, a police sergeant, "but one that happens a lot. A particular patrol officer has bad job habits, such as turning reports in late, being off the beat without permission, et cetera. Now that he is a supervisor, can he be effective? The problem surfaces when he must tell his officers to stop flaking off and do their jobs. They will think him a hypocrite for doing one thing and preaching another."

"Be open and honest with folks," a personnel director tells us. "The worst trouble I have seen people get into is when they get too 'cute' with the story, they get too 'cute' with the facts, and they do things that they would not be willing to share publicly. And that is the road to hell. Once you cross that threshold of *not* being up-front and honest about things, you are dead meat."

For supervisors to gain the confidence of their workers, they must be trustworthy—that is, consistently tell the truth, keep promises, protect confidences, and remain neutral in personal affairs as a matter of regular habit. Building the confidence of workers not only establishes rapport; it also builds their confidence in you, according to a recreation services manager.

In addition, one must be able to take criticism in the same way that it is given. Suggests an older supervisor:

Remind them that we are a team, not individuals in competing projects. At least once a week I get with my staff to do a review and constructive criticism session. We sit and discuss. This is a positive session. It doesn't get anyone down, but helps improve each as an individual and complete projects faster and easier. No one takes it like they're trying to get back at you. It has helped to better the program, to better our feelings about each other. Consequently, the work has been very productive. When criticism is pointed at me, I listen and take in what is said to me. My attitude is that they are making me a better person, which enables me to supervise them properly.

Letting people know that it is okay to disagree is important. "Let people know about disagreements," says a planning supervisor. "That is a sign of a good manager. Being open to criticism allows you to grow. If you cut off communication, you miss out on those good ideas and hurt yourself in the end."

Criticism has its place—especially constructive criticism. A fire department chief wryly observes, "Don't sit and complain about how things are run today, because tomorrow you may be in charge, and those complaints will come back to haunt you. If you want that job, don't bad-mouth the person who is doing it today."

To Summarize

One of the first hurdles facing new supervisors is to make a graceful transition from being a frontline worker to being in a position of authority over others. The transition from worker to supervisor can be quite a shock. Becoming a successful supervisor is more than just a new title, better pay, enhanced prestige, a private office, and perhaps some special privileges. What seems to sharply distinguish supervision from the previous job is that one's responsibility has changed—supervisors are not just responsible for their own work but for other people's work too. Supervisors are responsible for planning, organizing, staffing, directing, controlling, reporting, and budgeting to achieve the organization's goals.

Supervision means working *through others* to get the job done, not doing the work yourself or having others do the work as if they were you. In the process of working through others, supervisors take on many different roles to guide workers toward organizational goals.

To be effective requires technical, conceptual, and human relations skills. To develop the latter takes time, a sense of commonality with and an appreciation of workers, and personal integrity.

In all, successful supervision requires the development of new skills and abilities. The passion and intensity that has come from directing one's own work must now be transferred to the work of others. Through others, the work of supervision is accomplished.

Items for Reflection

1. What techniques might supervisors use to effectively work through others to achieve organizational goals?
2. When is directing the work of others preferable to working through others?
3. Describe examples of Mintzberg's interpersonal, informational, and decisional roles in your workplace.
4. Some management writers suggest that POSDCORB is a continuous process and others say it is not. Examine the rationale for both sides and give justifications for each argument.
5. What is the proper balance of technical, conceptual, and human expertise? Some argue that less technical and more conceptual skills are needed as one is promoted into the upper ranks of management.

2

Making the Transition Easier

The public sector supervisors we interviewed faced a number of similar problems when they first assumed the role of supervisor. The tactics presented here are a distillation of hundreds of good responses and many years of experience. While there was a range of answers, there was also a common foundation for action. How they dealt with these transition problems has been organized into three categories. The first is how to deal with inevitable changes in interpersonal relationships. The second is how others perceive you and how to be a credible supervisor. The chapter ends with suggestions for dealing with specific contemporary problems faced in the transition to becoming a supervisor.

About Friends and Former Co-Workers

One of the most troubling areas of adjustment in the transition from worker to supervisor is dealing with those people who used to be one's peers. "One of the most traumatic experiences I had while working at the Postal Service was the very first day I put on my tie," remembers one postal supervisor. "Putting on that tie separated me from my co-worker friends and placed me into a supervisor capacity. I was being put into the category of people that we (being clerks, subordinates) always talked badly about."

That seemingly simple change in roles has a profound effect on relationships, especially with friends and peers who suddenly become one's subordinates. "The biggest stress and strain that I had was when I made the transition from agent to supervisor," says a federal law enforcement supervisor. He explains:

You were a worker; now all of a sudden you are a supervisor. The people who were your friends, you used to sit down with and have a beer, go to dinner with, can't be any longer—the rules start changing immediately. It creates a complete change of lifestyle. It is the biggest pressure cooker you can imagine. When you went out with your buddies, you could criticize management and show your dislike of management roles . . . and all of a sudden you become one. Now you have to impose on your line of thinking—a management style—rather than the attitudes of working troops. It is a terrible and heavy transition with a great deal of pressure associated with it.

A particularly ticklish problem is evaluating the job performance of former friends and co-workers. "Being in the position of judging a person is always stressful," says Ruth

Ann Hageman, "even if you have employees who are 100 percent excellent. They are the ones who are judged, and you are the person who judges. That always sets a little distance between you and the others."

One solution suggested by a supervisor takes that distancing perhaps too far: "Sometimes I would feel uncomfortable when approaching people on work performance. These are people you know and who are your friends. Now I've learned to deal with that because it is not my fault, it is theirs." While there may be some validity in that statement, blame is not the issue in any performance evaluation. Hageman suggests a better approach: follow the personnel rules. "In some ways," she says, "the rules have dictates that are just common sense, but in other ways they are very specific on procedures that should be followed to be fair to employees—to give them the opportunity to grow and develop their skills in a positive way."

Friends Versus Being Friendly

Can a supervisor have subordinates as friends? One supervisor tells us that he was threatened with discipline by his own boss if he did not stop taking breaks and lunch with his subordinates. His supervisor thought that he was getting too friendly with his workers. The concern was not so much that he was on good terms with his subordinates, but that he was losing his objectivity—that is, losing his perspective on organizational goals, his ability to impartially evaluate performance, and his capacity to lead on the basis of rationality instead of favors. To be a successful supervisor, one has to be impartial and to appear not to favor one worker over another or workers over management.

According to the supervisors we talked with, there is little question that the transition from worker to supervisor means separating personal relationships from professional relationships. It often means placing a check on personal friendships because the appearance of impartiality and even-handed treatment is too important to risk losing the respect of your workers. Any hint that a supervisor is letting friends off easy or not expecting them to work to their full potential like everyone else will cost that supervisor what respect and loyalty he or she had already gained.

Although it is not surprising that those standing in opposition will withdraw their support deliberately to make life miserable for the new supervisor, what is ironic is that those being favored can just as easily withhold their consent. It is when they see that the supervisor needs them more than they need the supervisor that they realize how weak the supervisor has become. That is why some supervisors have few friendships with workers, both on and off the work site. In one case, one supervisor reports that he was only able to take up a friendship with a former co-worker after he had left the organization.

A public works supervisor points out that it is not easy to maintain a neutral or professional relationship. Favoritism can easily creep in. "I think you have to try to differentiate between the personal relationship and the professional relationship," he says. "But it's easier said than done. We tend to get along with people who think like we do, because those are the people we associate with. When we work with them, we naturally gravitate toward them. When we supervise, we tend to unconsciously favor those people who react the way we do to various circumstances. Somebody who does not think the way we do is starting out with a strike against them." The way to deal with this, he suggests, is "to make a conscious effort to be equitable in your distribution of both good and bad things in the supervisor position."

Divided Loyalties

Former co-workers will also question one's loyalty. Are you one of them, or a spy for management? "The subordinates assumed that my allegiance went to management despite the relationship that had been fostered with fellow co-workers," recalls a bus transit supervisor. In spite of mutually shared hopes and dreams as fellow co-workers, "workers you left behind tend to have the attitude that you are a turncoat," Linda Oravec, an executive director, points out. "You are no longer in their realm; therefore, you are the enemy."

To complicate matters, while workers are questioning the supervisor's loyalties, supervisors are also questioning the workers', according to an employment services supervisor. "In the transition, I lost friends because some became cold towards me. For example, they stopped discussing certain issues like co-workers' job performance because I became a part of management. Now when they do warm up to me, they just want to get information from me."

Advice on how to deal with divided loyalties was varied. Says one supervisor, "It took me a while. The way I came to grips with it [was] by deciding that I couldn't be one of the boys anymore. I couldn't please management *and* please the nonsupervisory people. You have to sever some very heavy ties sometimes." It takes time, too, adds Oravec. "It takes a while to adjust, maybe four to six weeks, maybe two months for some people. You need to be patient during the adjustment period. You need to relax."

"It is a hard thing to do," insists a regional planning supervisor, "to make sure subordinates understand that you are the boss and to be friendly at the same time. The thing is, they have to understand that they are accountable and you are responsible." It helps, another supervisor suggests, to treat your people like mature, professional individuals and not as if they are either friends or enemies.

Competitors and Predators

Confusion about where a supervisor's sentiments lie is but one of the reasons for tension between new supervisors and their former friends and co-workers. Resentment about the promotion may also lead to difficulty—co-workers thinking that they were equally, if not better, qualified to fill the position. Or there may be a cadre of workers who simply oppose the new supervisor because they feel that they have greater job knowledge, seniority, or both.

According to a recreation services manager, resentment can be dealt with effectively through an open discussion of the problem:

> The way I dealt with it was to acknowledge it right up front to the people when I was given the position. I acknowledged the situation with them and said it could be a problem. I told them I would work with

34

them any way that I could and be sensitive to that fact. We had a couple of conversations along the way. Then a couple of months later I could sense that there was a problem with one of the employees. I brought it back to them again and said I was sensing that it was a problem and we just talked about it.

Another supervisor recounts a similar story:

When I came to this city, there was a fellow who was assistant director of this department and still is. There were times when there was conflict between us. I brought him in and sat him down to talk about this conflict. I had transferred from out of state when I was hired for this job. I didn't know him from any-one else, so he had no reason to personally resent the fact that I got the job. We worked things out and I am still on a friendly basis with him.

If the problem persists, stronger measures may be needed. "There are two alternatives," says Kevin Hardy. "Either that person is supportive and understands the process and is happy for you and is a real friend. Or else they are passively or overtly aggressive and jealous about it. In the overt situation, it's pretty easy to just deal with it and say what happened. Try to get them to talk it through and see if they can deal with it. If they can't, then it's time for them to move on, because they lost and that's the way things worked out."

"If they are passive about it," he continues, "this is the person you need to be careful with. Somebody who is pas-sively aggressive (who won't be up-front with you), you probably won't find out about until a big milestone or objective-type achievement is about to be met. Then all of a sudden they let you down. Thirty minutes before you are supposed to be in front of the city council and a very critical piece of your presentation is missing." If one cannot prevent this situation by having the passive-aggressive person commit earlier and publicly to agree to goals, then one is put in a position of having to acknowledge an unworkable situation. Hardy suggests confronting the person. The solution in this case is to offer your help in finding this person another job. It does not have to be done with any animosity; it can, for example, be put in terms of doing the job altogether.

Another approach to dealing with friends, competitors, and predators is much more radical. According to Robert Hutchinson, a county facilities management supervisor, "It is complicated when people are pulled out of the ranks and made supervisors of the people in their own shop. The stories are rife with people who did not do well at all because they were supervising peers. So my advice is, if possible, be reassigned to a similar job assignment over a different group of people" or a different geographic area.

To some, of course, moving from a comfortable location and uprooting a family may seem too high a price to pay. However, there are definite advantages. "I think it is a lot easier on the new manager," says another supervisor, "if you supervise people that you did not associate with. You don't have those old habits, old relationships, and ties to overcome." It avoids awkward moments, suggests an environmental health supervisor, when you might have to say blunt things.

Self-Development

As new supervisors will quickly learn, there are always two sides to every problem. As the new supervisor sees his or her former friends and co-workers as problems, so do they see the neophyte supervisor as a problem. Knowing how to deal with former friends and co-workers is only part of it. New supervisors must also know how to deal with themselves—to look introspectively at their own makeup to identify potentially negative and nonproductive behaviors.

This used to be considered unimportant, because workers were simply supposed to follow orders. However, the tone that is set for the work unit is quite often a direct reflection of the character, values, and ambitions of the supervisor. To be effective, supervisors must be open to learning about themselves and others.

Be Knowledgeable

There are several aspects to being a knowledgeable supervisor. Supervision knowledge is not just about the technical aspects of the worker's job. You have to know your people and yourself, say veteran supervisors. "I think something really important for people who are just stepping into the supervisory role is to know their own strengths and weaknesses," says a small city recreation department supervisor. "You have to give some thought to your own supervisory style. Sometimes some styles sound really great on paper, but it is just not your way. Don't even attempt it. Just stay with what you are comfortable with and do the best you can with it."

"Get to know your workers," advises another. "These people will be working for you day in and day out. It is these people who will make or break the daily productivity goals. If the supervisor has a hard time dealing with people, or finds it difficult to tell someone to do something, then they don't belong in management." Remember, supervision is *working through others* to get the job done.

"You have to have a good knowledge of what you are capable of doing interpersonally with people," says Hardy, "but you also have to have a good grip on your organization's personnel policies and procedures." After all, it is hard to direct the work of others if you do not know the proper procedures for reorganization, assignment of work, and evaluating and rewarding performance.

Get Training

"Being a supervisor is a learning process," explains a city parks and recreation supervisor. "People aren't born to do it, although some people are better at it than others. You go out and get some training. It would be nice to get some training on the principles before you become a supervisor."

However, not everyone is prepared. "People often get promoted because they are good technicians," Cheryl Fruchter reminds us. "But when we promote them to supervisor, we fail to give them any training in supervising. Even though they know the work of the people they supervise, they don't have any supervisory skills, such as setting performance goals for their employees or [knowing] how to counsel them. In government there is often no training required when you become a supervisor. You have no skills, and yet it is expected that you are going to do a good job at it." Supervision is so different, indicates Hutchinson, that it might be considered a "foreign job assignment" for some.

Fruchter goes on to say, "Anyone being promoted into a supervisory position should have basic supervisory training, including doing performance evaluations, dealing with problems between employees, employee grievances, and setting policies for vacation and sick leave." These are areas that tend to be troublesome for new supervisors because they involve a showdown with workers. An over- or underuse of power by the supervisor can be disastrous, whereas a reasoned but firm stance will have the proper effect.

If one's organization does not provide training, one supervisor suggests letting "the organization send you to a seminar. In my experience, I had on-the-job training, and it was a trial-and-error process." If funds are not available, Hutchinson suggests that new supervisors go out and spend the money themselves. His argument is that one can get valuable information in a concentrated form and use it right away. Most training departments regularly receive brochures, pamphlets, and other advertisements from university and for-profit training programs.

If resources are limited, another strategy might be to seek the tutelage of a successful supervisor. A federal government supervisor tells how he did it: "When I decided that I wanted to join management, I selected two supervisors I wanted to act like. They had been in management for some time and had gained the respect of not only their subordinates but peers alike. I tried to model my management style to be like theirs. Try to pattern your style after them, but do not try to be that person."

Get Experience

There are formal and informal methods for gaining actual supervisory experience after obtaining training. "The Postal Service is good about allowing promising individuals the chance to be detailed to entry-level supervisor positions," says one supervisor who had been on a special duty assignment. "This was really important in that I could test my own managerial abilities and capacities for dealing with operations, other supervisors and superiors, and most importantly the workers assigned to my areas." He also reports that a temporary duty assignment was a good way for him to make sure that he really wanted to be a supervisor.

The process may be informal, according to Tim Vasquez. "It doesn't have to be a formal position like assistant supervisor. A supervisor can give a subordinate who he thinks has supervisor potential extra duties. For example, sending them to meetings in your place and putting them in charge of your duties when you are on vacation or away from the office."

Hutchinson suggests an even more proactive stance, a process he refers to as "pledging." "If I [am] going to go for the next job up the ladder, I've got to do extra work. I've got to start doing that job a bit at a time to bridge the gap. And I'd start six months to a year before I wanted the promotion because you just don't learn certain management skills overnight." For example, understanding a budget or being articulate in safety regulations is going to take time.

Learn from Mistakes

"The number one pressure," according to a labor relations manager for a large city, "is the pressure that we actually place on ourselves. The desire to hit the ground running and be an extremely competent and optimal kind of supervisor right off the bat is part of the competitive nature in us all. We all want to think we are the best at what we do and would like to be the best at what we do from day one. But the reality of the matter is that we are not."

Both Vasquez and Hutchinson advise aspiring supervisors to work closely with their bosses. "If you ask your supervisor to give you some tasks where failure is not such a big deal," says Hutchinson, "they can, in fact be your mentor and trainer—so that if you do fall down on the job, you know where your mistake was. You learn from that mistake, you press on, and you just don't do that mistake again. We all learn by mistakes."

It is okay to make mistakes, says Charles Marshall. "Don't be afraid to make mistakes. If you make a mistake, learn from it and go from there." Do not hide your mistakes, warns a personnel director. "Very few people get in serious trouble when sharing a screwup. But you sure get in a lot of trouble for not sharing it and then pretending it did not happen. It just does not work." Other supervisors suggested finding someone one can vent one's feelings with. Preferably select a superior or a fellow supervisor who can come to your aid when you are overloaded. Relying on a subordinate has its disadvantages. It may leave the other workers thinking that the supervisor is playing favorites, and it would not be possible to exchange certain duties and projects with subordinates, especially those requiring confidentiality. On the other hand, working with fellow supervisors can have its advantages. "Asking other supervisors what their departments do," says Barbara Baker, "not only helps coordination, but also develops a resource for later knowledge that can be accessed."

It Still Is Not Easy

The advice offered so far will undoubtedly prove to be useful in the long run, but the road to successful supervision is, as has been suggested before, a continuous learning experience. No single solution will fit all the possible situations and circumstances that new supervisors will find themselves in. One can expect to make a number of mistakes along the way. Although it is not always possible to come up with the most correct answer to complex problems, one can at least learn to ask the right questions.

On Acceptance

Can you live with rejection? New supervisors should not expect to be accepted by workers, fellow supervisors, and upper management until they have proven themselves—building trust always takes time. It is especially difficult for front-line supervisors, because they are usually caught between "a rock and a hard place," so to speak—neither workers nor management ever seem completely happy with what they do. Everyone has his or her own ideas, and no one is asking the neophyte supervisor. It is almost as though one were a messenger caught in a rut, bringing bad news first from one side and then from the other.

It is a difficult situation with which there may always be a certain level of discomfort. "I believe new supervisors stress out over being accepted," says a federal drug agent supervisor. "Learn to accept that there will be resentment and jealousy. I've learned that you cannot expect respect automatically just because of your title."

Certainly this does not mean that supervisors should ignore the feelings being expressed by others. What it does mean is that inexperienced supervisors need to develop a "thick skin." When concerns are expressed by workers or management, the complaints are often really about the position held and not directed at the person holding the position. Supervisors who take such concerns the wrong way are apt to compound the problem by holding a grudge or wanting to strike back at the complainers rather than looking for the underlying reasons for their unhappiness.

One supervisor rather whimsically notes, "If I didn't hear moaning and groaning, I'd be concerned." Indeed, if workers are not speaking up, one should be very much on guard because it probably means that communication has been cut off or broken down.

Family

Does your family understand and appreciate your emotional reactions to the job? One of the dangers of a stress-filled job is taking that job home with you. A labor relations supervisor observes, "Normally, management jobs in the real world are jobs that require you to commit a significant amount of time (especially in the beginning). That simply means you've got to sacrifice time. Time away from family; time away from friends. That is just something that is reality as far as a managerial situation is concerned." That pressure places a heavy burden on loved ones.

"But eventually," says another, "you come to the realization that worrying about it won't get the job done. You develop follow-up procedures to get things done and don't take it home with you.

Although family or close, non–work-related friends form a support system for you, they may never completely understand the trials and tribulations of supervision. If the supervisor becomes burned-out and is unable to separate work from home, the effects may be felt throughout the family constellation.

Diversity and Difference

According to predictions, tomorrow's workplace is going to be more diverse—a greater cultural mix, education range, age span, and variety of family arrangements. "To be effective now as a supervisor," observes a personnel director, "people should have an appreciation for other people, for their differences, for all the differences they bring to the workplace. If you don't appreciate the people as actual value, then you don't have much of a chance. You've got to take care of your folks."

Diversity is a complex issue that often evokes strong emotional responses and few solid answers. However, it is better to ask a troubling question and start a dialogue than never to ask and allow feelings to fester. For example, should workers be allowed to speak to each other in their native tongue when it excludes others in the office? Should single parents be allowed time off to care for sick children, especially when the children cannot go to day care when ill? Should workers be allowed time off to care for their elderly parents? Should same-gender spouses or partners be given the same benefits as heterosexual counterparts?

Limited Resources

How do you get more with less? As mentioned earlier, a seemingly perpetual problem in public sector organizations is lack of resources. Revenue shortfalls result in reduced services and postponed routine maintenance of buildings and equipment, preclude repair or replacement of broken equipment, and prevent the purchase of equipment, such as desktop computers, that would increase productivity. User fees, privatization, equipment leases, public/private sector partnerships, and productivity programs are some of the methods proposed to overcome limited fiscal resources. However, each comes with attached costs. For example, user fees raise the ire of many taxpayers, upset elected officials who fear another taxpayers' revolt, and, due to surreptitious transfer of funds, do not always lead to the reinstatement or continuance of services. Privatization, equipment leases, and public/private sector partnerships may also have unintended consequences, such as the creation of another bureaucracy to monitor the joint ventures. Postponing routine maintenance has the short-term effect of saving funds but increases the probability of more costly equipment replacement later and subjects the organization to questions about liability if people are injured as a result of faulty equipment.

Time is also a limited resource and a precious commodity. Time can be mismanaged easily. For example, public organizations need to be responsive. However, a reactive management approach can easily lead to putting out brush fires without ever examining or evaluating underlying problems, much less spending the needed time on tasks important to the overall mission of the organization. Although accountability is important, time can also be wasted by redundant reporting systems and excessive paperwork. In one social work agency, it took sixteen forms to place a child into foster care and eighteen more to remove the child.

The issue of limited resources is not confined just to adequate funding and time but also includes human resources—competent and motivated people. Unfortunately, one consequence of a continuing onslaught by the media and many political candidates against "bureaucrats" and "red tape" is that potential candidates are discouraged from seeking employment in the public sector. Less-than-competitive salaries, benefits, and perquisites are only one aspect of this portrayal of a dull, gray, unchallenging career as a paper pusher. The result, of course, is that supervisors have fewer qualified job applicants from whom to choose.

"If you've got bad people," says a supervisor, "you're in serious trouble. Life is so wonderful when you have a good staff. They do things. You can take the day off, and they won't screw up. The worst nightmare is bad, incompetent people. Or even worse, people who will hide things from you and not let you know they screwed something up."

To Summarize

The road from worker to supervisor is full of hazards, ranging from people who said they were your friends but were not to a turbulent and changing work world. The advice offered in this chapter addresses some of the problems faced. However, it is not always possible to anticipate every situation that will come along. What may be more important is being able to recognize a problem when one does occur and then asking the right questions. By making the appropriate inquiries and involving others in the process, a supervisor will be able to come up with better answers.

Items for Reflection

1. Describe some of the problems encountered in the transition from worker to supervisor and suggest some solutions that might work.
2. Explain how you would deal with former co-workers who are now your subordinates.
3. Explain why performance evaluation, resolving interpersonal conflict between workers, grievances, vacation schedules, and sick leave policies are problem areas for new supervisors.
4. Hutchinson and Baker list several problem areas for supervisors. Does one have the better list? Develop your own list of issues. Explain why they are important.

Baker's List

- Developing new peer relationships
- Developing relationships with superiors
- Delegating work
- Developing trust
- Performance evaluations

Hutchinson's List

- Discipline
- Hiring
- Planning
- Being an intermediary between workers and management

Part Two

KEY SUPERVISORY SKILLS AND RESPONSIBILITIES

3

Decision Making— Making the Right Choices

Decision making, the process of choosing an alternative from a number of possible alternatives, is not as easy as it sounds. Supervisors are under constant pressure to make good decisions: which work process will be the most effective, which work method is more efficient, what approach to motivation should be used, how should limited resources be allocated, when should discipline be used. Not only are the problems complex, but the decisions supervisors make affect many more lives and careers than their own. It is no longer a question of satisfying personal wants and desires. Much more is at stake.

Workers depend on their supervisors to make decisions that are consistent, equitable, and fair. Upper management wants choices made that improve the efficiency and the productivity of work units. The organization expects its supervisors to be innovative and creative in solving problems. Meanwhile, public policy makers, the media, and the public are all too ready to question the soundness of every decision made. As Ruth Ann Hageman puts it, the challenge is to "try to do it better, do it smarter, do it more efficiently, and do it with fewer resources."

Decision making can be particularly difficult for the beginning supervisor for a variety of reasons. "New supervisors tend to err on the conservative side," says one supervisor. In the opinion of another, new supervisors often act too hastily without adequate information. A third suggests that new supervisors take too long to reach a decision or even to realize that there is a problem. Yet another experienced supervisor suggests that new supervisors are fearful that they might offend others.

Decision making is a skill that can be learned and one that improves with experience. "When you are a neophyte, you apply rules and regulations—the process of decision making is clear cut," says J. D. Sandoval, a planning director. "When you gain experience, you begin to take into account political aspects and the impact your decision is going to have on other departments. You need to be aware of the whole picture in order to make good decisions."

This chapter, then, is designed to help new supervisors become aware of the "whole picture" of problem solving so they can make more effective decisions. We begin by examining the traditional problem-solving model and by suggesting ways to make it work better. This is followed by a discussion of two opposing viewpoints on the scope of decision making in the public sector. Finally, several techniques for improving decision making are explored.

Five Steps to Solving Problems

When faced with a problem, almost invariably supervisors turn to the same model of problem solving. More or less, the model consists of the following steps:

1. Identifying the problem
2. Considering and weighing alternatives
3. Picking the best option
4. Implementing the decision
5. Evaluating the impact

It is believed by many that by systematically following these five steps, successful decisions will be reached. However, this model also assumes that decision makers have complete and accurate information about the situation in question, as well as the time to logically and rationally analyze the possible ramifications of each option. According to the supervisors we interviewed, rarely is this the case. Conditions usually dictate that decisions be made with limited knowledge and with little time for careful analysis.

One frequently heard word of advice is to rely on intuition and experience (that is, experience related to the problem being addressed and experience in decision making itself). It is clear that the development of such a "sixth sense" is not haphazard. Let us examine each of the five steps to problem solving and discover how intuition is developed.

Identifying the Problem

Problems are often very complex. Imagine, for the moment, being the supervisor of a worker who rides the bus and has a history of being tardy for work. When asked, the worker says the bus is rarely on schedule. The explanation makes sense, so you talk with the worker about bus schedules, taking an earlier bus, or perhaps even carpooling with others. Over the next few weeks, the worker continues to show up late. The worker looks unhappy. Because the worker's performance is only average, you decide that the real cause might be that the worker does not like something about work. You spend time discussing what job tasks and activities the worker likes and dislikes. More time passes, and the worker is still coming in late. You ask around and find out that the worker has young children. You deduce that the tardiness might be caused by overly sleepy children or problems with the baby-sitter—understandable circumstances to be sure. When confronted, however, the worker refuses to talk about baby-sitting arrangements. The worker announces that day-care arrangements are not job related and that there is an attorney who will gladly talk to you about a civil suit for job harassment. Finally, you calm the worker down and reach an agreement about flexible hours—only to find a few days later that others in your unit are ready to file a grievance against you for preferential treatment of one worker.

What is the moral of the story?

First, it is important to identify the correct problem. Quite often the apparent problem is different from the real problem. Failure to determine the underlying cause of a problem means that valuable time, energy, and resources may be spent working on the wrong aspect of the problem or merely alleviating symptoms. How the problem is defined affects each successive step of the problem-solving model. It especially affects the solutions being considered. In the above case, the apparent solution would be different depending on whether the problem was viewed as one of tardiness, productivity, job satisfaction, day care, liability, or fairness.

How does one make sure that the right problem has been identified? A variety of approaches can be taken. One supervisor suggests consulting an expert, because experts can provide important information and facts. But a planning supervisor warns, "Don't be influenced by only one person's opinion, or panic. That person's opinion may be based on too little or wrong information." As an alternative, the personnel director of a small city advises, "I sometimes call other department heads for the history of past decisions on similar matters. By inquiring about past events, I am providing myself with information from which I can make a better decision." Along these same lines, getting as much information as possible to identify the root problem and root cause may mean asking those closest to the problem. One frequently overlooked source is the people actually doing the job. "Sometimes employees know more about specific things than you," says a physical plant supervisor with twenty-five years of experience. "Listen to them!"

The second moral of the story is that it is important to understand the context within which the problem occurs. Problems rarely occur in isolation from other problems. It is not uncommon to find different problems intertwined, or the cause of one problem linked to another

55

problem. In addition, solutions have ramifications for other activities and may be the cause of further problems. That is, every decision a supervisor makes will have repercussions beyond the original intent. In the example just given, the supervisor's decision to allow flex time for one worker's situation affected the larger group. That supervisor should not be surprised to hear concerns and complaints from other supervisors and workers in other units as well.

One way to gain perspective on the context surrounding a problem is to remember who you are working for. According to Charles Marshall, "If you are working for the fire department management, your job is to carry out a set of objectives that is basically dictated by fire department policy." At the same time, however, it is also important to assess the overall environment. "Look at the big picture and all the ramifications," says a recreation manager. "Make sure you are not looking through a small hole."

A popular way to avoid identifying the wrong problem is by using group problem-solving methods. The more people who understand that there is a problem, the less likely it is that there will be questions later—that is, what the problem is, if any. We will return to group decision making later. For now, suffice it to say, as several supervisors put it—"two heads are better than one."

Considering and Weighing Alternatives

The second step in the problem-solving process is to generate and then evaluate and prioritize various alternative solutions to the problem. Ideally, one wants to create as many plausible solutions as possible and discuss the advantages and disadvantages of each. The chances of picking the right solution are greater when one has taken the time to be thorough. Hasty thinking often leads to easy solutions rather than to solutions that link cause to effect.

It sounds easy, but difficulties may arise. "The difficulty," a public works supervisor complains, "is getting enough information in the time you need to make the decision. Often you are pressed to make a decision without sufficient research, without enough background information, or without understanding the full ramifications of it. Ten years later it comes back to haunt you."

Even when there is time, it is not always possible to speak with much certainty about the conceivable consequences of a given alternative. A supervisor we talked with gave an example: a governmental organization decided to build its own electrical cogeneration plant as a way to keep electric bills from rising. The equipment was installed in three locations, but the results were far from what was predicted. Because this was fairly new technology, the contractor was often in the dark about what needed to be done. As a result, the units were down more than was expected. To make matters worse, it turned out that even at maximum efficiency the units were not designed to produce the needed energy. The project ended up costing more and producing less than was envisioned. In this instance, what was anticipated was far from what happened— not necessarily because of poor planning, but rather because things can and do go wrong.

Another difficulty is that we have a tendency to consider only a limited number of alternatives. Simon (1976)

57

described this phenomenon as *satisficing*—a term that he coined by combining *satis*factory and suf*fice*. The term suggests that we do not search for optimal, comprehensive solutions to problems. We conduct only a limited search for alternatives, and when we find a satisfactory solution that meets minimum standards of sufficiency, we stop considering other alternatives.

In the public sector, political reality tends to limit the choices of alternatives that are considered. Political pressures may alter both the priority of alternative solutions and the desirability of resultant outcomes. As an example, consider the case of the California State Lottery. With revenues dwindling (as revenues of state lotteries nationwide have historically done), California lottery officials planned to redesign the biweekly Lotto Game. A number of solutions were suggested: increase or decrease the number of drawings per week, design a new game, artificially increase the size of the winnings by diverting funds, and so on. Arguing that their surveys indicated players wanted to win more frequently (even if the prizes were smaller), the lottery director decided to increase the odds of winning as a way to increase sales and revenues. Faced with a budgetary crisis, the governor showed his displeasure with the decision by firing the lottery director and laying off staff.

Finally, funding limitations affect the level of resources available to implement programs. For many years, the State of Arizona has been the only state that has refused to implement the Medicaid program. Because it is a federal requirement for all states receiving funds for Aid to Families with Dependent Children (AFDC) to have a Medicaid program, Arizona passed the required legislation to have the program on the books. However, Medicaid has never been included in the state budget.

Although consideration of alternatives may be somewhat circumscribed at times, that does not mean that an effort should not be made to explore as many alternatives as possible within the constraints imposed. "Make a list of pros and cons," suggests a personnel analyst. "Consider the repercussions of a yes or no answer. Whom will it affect? Will it affect morale? If you have the opportunity, bounce your ideas of possible solutions off of co-workers or other supervisors. It can be helpful to say, 'This is my problem, this is what I'm thinking of doing—what do you think?' This way, you can get someone else's fresh look at it."

Another supervisor advises, "A supervisor should consult other managers and top employees for ideas. Be open to innovative ideas. Think through all possible avenues of approach. A good decision maker will not hesitate to change an approach."

Since we know that time is a critical factor in generating a given quantity and quality of alternatives, one supervisor suggests anticipating problems and solutions. "Try to foresee when you are going to have to make the decision, and all the time prior to that you can use to gather information. You can talk to others who have been faced with the same decision and maybe talk to those who have done things that you intend to do. Then when the time comes you will be better prepared."

Picking the Best Option

The supervisors we interviewed expressed concern about the speed with which decisions are made and about the purpose or intent underlying the decisions. Let us examine each of these in turn.

First, taking too long to reach a decision leaves workers with the wrong impression. "The important thing is not to be indecisive," says Jon Torchia, a fire captain. "Your staff looks to you to be decisive and criticizes you for being wishy-washy," a school administrator adds. A personnel supervisor warns, "Don't hesitate for so long that you end up making the decision by default. You should consciously choose one way or the other rather than do nothing. Otherwise, all of a sudden the decision is made because something had to be done."

In a way, of course, failing to make a decision is one way of making a decision. "Don't be afraid," says a supervisor in a metropolitan transit district. "Take a chance and face the responsibilities!" "It is better to make the decision and find out it is wrong than to make it by default," adds another. By not making decisions, "This means that you are not managing or providing leadership," says a small town personnel director. "You must be proactive within your organization. You must set acceptable standards."

Slow decision making may have many origins. If you spend too much time getting data, "you tend to become a roadblock to the decision-making process," Robert Nelson, public works director of Encinitas, California, observes. "This can cause you to back into a decision that you may not otherwise make." On the same topic Robert Hutchinson of the County of San Diego advises, "Every supervisor must realize that they are going to have to make decisions on incomplete data. You cannot allow yourself to be drawn into the morass of paralysis of analysis."

A hesitant decision may also be caused by fear of being wrong. "I make a lot of decisions regarding undercover situations," a law enforcement supervisor tells us. "You stay up nights wondering about the guy you had do real deep undercover. Whether they are going to pull out or if something will go wrong . . . heavy, heavy decisions. In time you learn to make a decision and leave it—good, bad, or indifferent. The decision has been made. Leave it alone—don't second-guess it." Or, as another supervisor aptly puts it, "It is not up for replay."

One makes the best decision based on the information available. "If the decision happens to not work out, the decision maker made a well-reasoned decision at the time it was made with whatever available information was accessible," says Barbara Baker, a supervisor of public fiduciaries. "If one gets additional information sometime later that proves the decision was wrong, it was still the best decision one could have made at the time."

"One must be able to make decisions whether they turn out good or bad," argues Torchia. "You are never going to be safe, sound, or secure in every decision you make," a large city labor relations manager says in agreement. "So you can't be afraid to make a decision. You have to make decisions and understand that in hindsight not every one that you make will be the best. As long as you learn from it, you will continue to grow and be better prepared to cope with similar situations."

If you do make a bad decision, be flexible enough to change. "The best thing to do is say 'I blew it,'" explains a buildings division supervisor. "Admit your mistake and try not to do it again." Another way to look at it is suggested by a supervisor at a university campus: "Since organizations are not static but fluid, you will not always make the right decision. It depends on the situation. So it is not an issue of right and wrong, but an issue of the best solution under the circumstances."

Some new supervisors reach decisions too slowly, but the supervisors we spoke to also expressed concern that some new supervisors might pick solutions too quickly. A number of interviewees stated that it is important to get as much information as possible before making a decision. "Don't be too hasty," one fire chief remarks. "It's not imperative that because somebody asks a question that you have to give them an answer immediately. Do your research, follow established guidelines and procedures, and talk to people about the ramifications and whether or not you have the authority to make that decision. Don't jump in with both feet just because you feel that you are the manager. You can bury yourself flat doing this." In the opinion of one school principal, "[Say] 'Let me think it over and I'll give my decision tomorrow before the end of the day.' People tend to respect you more when a little time is put into the decision."

Emotions can also play a role in making a decision too quickly. "Don't make decisions in anger," a physical plant manager observes, "especially quick ones concerning employees." The personnel director of a large city agrees. "Once you are emotionally involved, you are going to make mistakes. You are going to screw it up—big time. People have to learn how to step back and get out of the emotion of it." As children, our parents always told us to think before acting, but it is difficult to plan it out and not overreact when the pressure is on. A point that Leroy Brady acknowledges. "The decisions that have come back to bite me are ones that were made from an emotional standpoint," he says.

The point here is not that a supervisor should put aside feelings—an impassioned attitude about work, people, and organization play a role in successful supervision—but that fairness and due process often require putting self-indulgent feelings on hold for the good of the group and the decision itself.

In addition to picking a solution too quickly or too slowly, one can make a decision for the wrong reasons. The seasoned supervisors we queried had some excellent suggestions for picking the best possible alternative from the ones that are available. The safest course of action when in doubt is, of course, to follow established policy and procedures, according to a parks and recreation manager. "Then your decision is already documented for you. In a bureaucracy, many of your decisions can be made by applying procedures that have been enforced in situations that have come up in the past."

However, a good decision is much more than following precedence and staying within given rules and regulations. Hutchinson puts it this way: "A decision is the action step of a plan that has been well thought out. As long as you keep heading towards your goal, you get to the next camp. If all of your decisions are aimed towards your next objective of the goal, they are going to be on a route, a plan." One public works director voices a similar theme. "Don't ever make a decision favoring short-term goals which negate a long-term goal." In other words, says a recreation department manager, "Don't be rigid on rules, policy, and procedures. Be flexible when making decisions so that you come out with the best outcome. The main thing is to have it benefit what you are deciding on, rather than restraining and restricting."

This is important advice, because there are different types of goals in the public sector: least cost, shortest time, minimum inconvenience, fairness, justice, and equity, to name a few. Depending on the overall goal, the best choice may be defined differently. As one supervisor puts it, besides knowing the facts and the background information, "Know what you want, what your superiors expect of you, and what employees expect."

One way to clarify the underlying purpose of a decision, according to Barbara Baker, is to think of the worst possible disaster that would result from the decision. It is advice well worth considering, because it is sometimes easier to conjure up the priorities in a worst-case scenario than to rank order the positive reasons for a decision. In addition, this approach is designed to counter the all-too-human tendency to want to believe that our decisions are omnipotent and infallible. Thus, it is a way of testing our assumptions. Although one should not second-guess a decision *after* it is made, raising questions *before* the decision is reached ensures that there is a match between the alternative chosen and the intended purpose or goal.

What if one does not have the foggiest idea what to decide? A personnel director in a large metropolitan area suggests simply asking for help. She believes that saying "I don't know" and asking for help are two of the greatest challenges facing new supervisors.

Implementing the Decision

Once the choice has been made, a plan of action must be developed to put the decision into action. Resources must be gathered, timetables for completion set up, duties assigned, and accountability systems installed. As in the other steps in the decision-making model, things can go awry in the implementation phase. According to Hutchinson, "You can have a good decision that is poorly implemented or a well-implemented decision that does not support the plan."

Two suggestions for avoiding these problems were emphasized by the supervisors. First, says Hageman, "The implementation has to be consistent with the purpose." This first suggestion is fairly straightforward. "You can hit a target with a rifle shot," says Hutchinson. "Or you can hit a target with a carom shot. You can hit the target with a mortar shot way up high and down below. Or you can walk over to the target. Different paths, different speeds, different techniques, but you are still aiming at the target."

Second, those working on the project need to be involved. This suggestion requires some thought. In many instances, implementation means that others will be involved in carrying out the plan of action. Studies by Vroom and Yetton (1973) indicate that implementation of a decision is easier if all involved understand and accept the decision. When the decision involves highly technical questions (for example, determining eligibility for services), those involved are likely to go along if the quality of the decision is good. That is, the focus is on how well the problem is understood and whether there is sufficient information to make a good decision. However, in other instances, such as deciding who will have to work overtime, the acceptance and commitment of those involved becomes critical to the success of the decision. This means that if conflict among participants is likely to result from the decision, they ought to be involved in making the decision.

Related to the issue of keeping everyone (line and support staff) informed is the idea of timing. Because it is not always possible to involve workers in every decision that affects them, supervisors must sometimes use an alternate strategy of involvement. "Making good decisions is a matter of timing," explains a veteran school district administrator. "Sometimes a supervisor waits to announce a decision; other times a decision is implemented relatively quickly. This is not a Perry Mason television show. Everyone should know what is going on." The real secret is knowing when to fully or only partially involve workers.

Evaluating the Impact

The final step in this decision-making model is to evaluate whether the chosen alternative is accomplishing the intended purpose. Feedback can be obtained in many different ways: through informal talks with those involved, or through formal staff meetings, reporting systems, audits, and performance evaluations. Whatever the method, the purpose is to gather sufficient information so that one can decide whether to continue the plan of action, to adjust it, or to begin the problem-solving process all over again. Says Baker, "Supervisors must know when to say that the decision did not work, accept it, modify it, and feel comfortable in changing the decision."

A supportive upper management that believes that a decision can be wrong and can be subject to later change is a key to effective evaluation. Consider the case of an office that decided that telephone messages should be put on computer rather than written on paper. Staff members were trained and the system was implemented. Soon thereafter complaints arose. The receptionist thought it was taking longer to pass messages along. It turned out that she was writing the messages down, then entering them on the computer later. Those reading the messages were printing them out instead of reading them on-screen and answering them directly. Tensions rose when the office supervisor forced the receptionist to make the system work rather than modifying the experiment or terminating it. The office supervisor's rationale for not making a recommendation to change the new message system was that the next level of management might misinterpret criticism and take it personally rather than professionally. By not having open avenues for feedback, resources were wasted and emotions frayed.

The Scope of Decision Making

In a classic piece published in 1959, Charles Lindblom described two very different approaches to decision making in the public sector: the rational-comprehensive approach and incrementalism (affectionately known as "the science of muddling through"). A rational-comprehensive approach to decision making has the broadest scope. In this approach, a problem is thoroughly analyzed to understand the underlying cause, all logical solutions are examined thoroughly, the effectiveness of possible solutions may be quantified as statistical probabilities, and a cost-benefit analysis may be employed to rank choices. The optimal solution may have a profound effect not only on how the problem is solved, but also on how it is defined.

The social policies of presidents John F. Kennedy and Lyndon Johnson, which were designed to eliminate poverty and its effects, are typical of this approach. Rather than sustaining the subsistence of poor families through welfare and unemployment payments, they addressed the underlying causes of poverty. Programs were started to increase affordable housing, to end job discrimination, to enhance the education of disadvantaged children through Head Start programs, and to train unskilled workers for better paying jobs.

In contrast to the rational-comprehensive approach, which seeks a single comprehensive solution and defines a good decision as the most efficient and effective means to the desired end, incrementalism is a succession of smaller, circumscribed decisions. That is, only a limited number of politically viable alternatives are considered. Sometimes important values, goals, and outcomes are neglected. In the final analysis, the definition of a good decision is measured by how much agreement can be generated. Thus, a good incremental decision, while not necessarily accomplishing the goal, saves the decision from outright rejection and opposition. As long as there is a modicum of agreement, the goal will eventually be achieved through a succession of subsequent incremental decisions. As a result, America's social welfare policy takes on a patchwork, mosaiclike quality—for example, limited job training programs for only the hard-core unemployed, short-term demonstration projects of limited scope, or affordable housing for select targeted populations.

Lindblom's argument was that the rational-comprehensive approach was intellectually logical, but doomed to failure because it ignored political reality. In the heated battle over pressing priorities, a rational-comprehensive approach forces decision makers to make hard choices and take sides. Whenever a rational-comprehensive approach is taken, valuable assets are diverted from one priority to another. Because of limited resources, favored programs receive funding and lower-priority programs may be scrapped. What the rational-comprehensive approach does not allow for is the lifeblood of politics: compromise. In a sense, incrementalism recognizes that it is more important to remain a part of the political agenda than to be absolutely right.

Supervisors, of course, use both approaches when making decisions. "The public sector is very complicated," says a supervisor we interviewed. "Through experience you find that it has a much broader range of questions than you would have thought coming out of school. Someone might ask something that seems like it is off the wall, but as you get familiar with the public sector you start understanding the themes which are important to public officials, and those become important to you as a manager." As new supervisors gain experience, they come to realize when it is generally more appropriate to use the rational-comprehensive approach rather than the "science of muddling through." Here is what other experienced supervisors have to say about making that choice.

"The rational-comprehensive approach is absolutely necessary," insists Hageman. "You have to have a larger picture and always ask 'What is the purpose of what we are doing.'" "In my business," adds a personnel director, "it has to be rational-comprehensive because you have to know where you are going at the end. Our plans are a year long at a minimum. We have another which is a five-year program. We are not Communists doing five-year plans, but you have to think big, rational, long-term. We had better know where we are going over the long haul. No one likes to be short-term, incrementally led—unless they are brand new trainees. Then it is a little different."

"Probably in practice," says Gregory Cantor, "incremental decision making gets utilized because the rational-comprehensive approach takes so long. Especially in the 'gray areas' incrementalism dominates." A small-city redevelopment director tells us how she hired a company to do what appeared to be a small project having to do with toxic

70

waste on a development site. It turned out to be a major project involving requests for proposals. "Sometimes," she says, "you don't understand the real problem until you have taken that initial incremental approach."

Baker both agrees and disagrees with the above statements. Her approach is similar to the mixed-scanning approach advocated by Amatai Etzioni (1967), a prominent sociologist, who questioned Lindblom's incrementalism–rationalism dichotomy. "When dealing with a major policy decision," Baker asserts, "the rational model should be used. Incrementalism deals with operational decision making." That is, one uses the rational-comprehensive approach to understand what could be and the incremental approach to move toward the goal. Not surprisingly, the secret to successfully using a mixed-scan approach is to not lose sight of the goal as one increments along.

A public works manager points out that the approach depends on the type of organization one is working for. A rational-comprehensive approach is more suited to what he terms a "nonprovincial" organization. Incrementalism seems to fit better with a "provincial" organization. "Provincials," he says, "are a much more difficult situation to deal with because they typically have the attitude that they have done it a particular way, it works, and why should we do it better. They are satisfied and comfortable, just like an old shoe. They consider it successful. Even though in most cases it is very inefficient, it works for the job that is getting done. To try to turn that type of a system around is extremely difficult."

Improving Decision Making

One of the most important things new supervisors can learn is to involve their subordinates in the decision-making process. "I feel that having your employees participate in the decision-making process is very important to your current and future success as a supervisor," a supervisor in a gas and electric utility reveals to us. "This is especially important when you are trying to implement new programs or projects. You need to have the employees 'buy in.' Remember, as a supervisor, you get most of your work done through people." Improved decision making, then, has subordinates participating in the decision-making process.

Brainstorming is a technique that was developed in the 1950s by Madison Avenue advertising firms to generate ideas. The technique is useful for getting input at each stage of the decision-making process. The ground rules are simple. Participants are asked to generate as many ideas as they can on a particular topic or to address a specific issue—the more ideas the better. Participants are encouraged to "piggyback" their ideas, that is, to add to the ideas of others. Criticism of ideas is prohibited, since any negative remarks might stifle creativity. The group facilitator's role is to record these ideas, to encourage input, and to prevent the premature critiquing of suggestions.

Reaching a group consensus about which ideas are best can be accomplished through several different methods. The *Delphi Technique* was developed in the 1950s by the

Rand Corporation, a think tank. The technique suggests that statistical averaging of experts' judgments can improve the accuracy of forecasting technological changes and avoid problems (for example, premature concurrence seeking, a shift toward a more risky solution, diffusion of responsibility, and leadership bias) often associated with traditional group interaction. This method was adopted by the defense industry to reach consensus in problem identification and solution as the U.S. Navy debated the goals and purposes of the first Polaris submarines. A number of experts were consulted individually about the goal of a weapon system that could launch intercontinental ballistic missiles yet be virtually undetectable because the delivery system would be mobile and underwater. Designing the system as a weapon of last resort versus one of first choice would have a tremendous impact on whether there were single or multiple warheads, conventional or nuclear armament, and a focus on speed, endurance, or stealth. The experts were asked to evaluate and then rank the purpose of the Polaris system. The responses were collected and aggregated. Preferences could be determined from the statistical average that resulted. If the results had been confusing or the alternatives still unclear, a refined survey would have been sent to the individual experts so they could vote again. Once the correct problem was identified, the Delphi Technique could then be used to reach consensus about various alternative strategies that might be used to reach the goal.

The *Nominal Group Technique* (NGT) is very similar to the Delphi Technique, except that there is interaction among the group members (Delbecq, Van de Ven, and Gustafson, 1975). A typical NGT session begins with brainstorming. The ideas produced are then consolidated into a number of smaller categories. Members are free to give their reasons for why ideas are linked, but they are not allowed to evaluate the items negatively. The voting is done in the group through a secret ballot. Each person ranks all of the choices. If there is no clear mathematical consensus, several rounds of voting may occur. Lower-ranked items may be eliminated in each round, leaving members to vote on the remaining higher-ranked items.

By far, the most frequently mentioned approach was *Participatory Decision Making*. The supervisors who spoke with us showed a remarkable sophistication in using this technique. They had a number of good reasons for including as much subordinate input as possible in each step of the problem-solving process. For instance, participation often means greater commitment. "It is important to have your staff involved," a recreation services supervisor states. "I think it helps them buy into the decision that is made. It makes them feel like part of the team and puts value on them because you respect their opinion. That says a lot. I think it makes them work harder. It makes them more committed to their job." Failure to include people makes them "feel slighted and their self-esteem suffers," a long-range planning supervisor concludes. It can lead to an "us-versus-them" attitude.

According to Hageman, "If they are given a mission statement that I wrote, then it is not *our* mission, it is *mine*." And that can make a big difference regarding whether subordinates will advocate for their supervisor's decision, go that extra step to accomplish the task, or give the supervisor feedback and information about potential barriers and pitfalls. Indeed, many a program or project has failed for want of broad-based support. As Mauro Garcia, an organization effectiveness specialist, states, "If people really aren't brought in on a decision, they can fight you all the way." Agreeing readily, personnel management supervisor Daniel Del Castillo contends, "Decisions that are good are always achieved in a cooperative environment. Decisions that are viewed as unilateral, personal, or secretive will most likely be resisted, undermined, or ignored."

Participation can also help the manager to see the "big picture," which is so critical in the decision-making process. "I don't always see the big picture," admits Torchia. "I like each person to lend his or her expertise." The personnel director of a large city apparently agrees. "You put a problem before a group of equal participants and you will get a better decision than if you just do it yourself. At times I think people are nuts when they present their position, but when you hear their rationale they think of something you never thought of."

"For managers not to seek the input or the feedback of their subordinates is the worst mistake that could be made in terms of expecting that anything positive will come out as a finished product in your organization," a labor relations manager insightfully observes. "No manager has a thumb or forefinger on the pulse beat of every operation within the organization, division, or whatever it might be."

In spite of the advantages of participatory decision making, it must be used with caution. "You have to know where to draw the line," insists Kevin Hardy. "There are certain times when decisions in a participative process tend to go outside the bounds of the issues at hand. They tend to bring on peripheral issues which make it more difficult to come to a conclusion. You need to be open and creative in getting ideas, but at a certain point you have to say, 'That's enough, let's work on these and go on to the next thing and put that behind us.'"

In addition to knowing when to limit the participation, Hardy goes on to say, supervisors must realize that certain topics for discussion are more appropriate than others for participatory decision making. "Participation is appropriate in any type of administrative, operational type of decision. Like how are we going to produce a budget from a tactical standpoint? Who is going to do what? Who is going to get which budgets? How are we going to run it between the clerical staff, and how are we going to get it to a printed final format? These things are perfect for participative decision making." But, he warns, "Things that are *not* open to the participative process are things like personnel decisions: hiring decisions, relations between yourself and a particular subordinate, and what type of discipline you are going to take upon this individual—absolutely not participatory."

Even those things peripherally related to personnel matters, such as pay, bonuses, types of leave given, and when leave is taken, for example, may be unsuitable for participatory decision making. Because people in the workplace may be sensitive to criticism and to how rewards are allocated, the mishandling of these matters can easily lead to interpersonal conflict and lower morale. As one supervisor puts it, "There are just some decisions that you cannot take a vote on and be democratic about it."

The confidential nature of some personnel decisions, however, does not mean that subordinates should be uninformed. Rather, it may be appropriate at certain times to keep subordinates informed about the reasons behind personnel decisions. One supervisor believes that this tactic is acceptable when used to counter untrue rumors and to reinforce the integrity of the personnel system rather than to embarrass the employees involved.

Although certain decisions and information may be confidential and not for general consumption, a supervisor must use caution before concluding that subordinates lack sufficient information to be included in participatory decision making. In an interesting twist, one supervisor in environmental health states that while it is not appropriate for other subordinates to be involved in disciplinary matters, the subject of the discipline certainly should be an active participant. "Last week I went through a disciplinary action," he recalls. "I asked the person, 'If you were in my place, what would you do?'" His reason for including the worker, he says, is "to make them accountable."

On the same subject, a public information supervisor believes, "If the decision is going to affect your work personally and they don't understand the reason for the decision that is being made, then it should be explained in detail."

Preparing people was also the message from Cheryl Fruchter:

> Sometimes there is information that you cannot actually pass on to them. Because they are not privy to that information, they could not make a good decision. However, I think you still try to have them participate as much as possible. Over a period of time you make sure that your employees understand how what they do fits in with the other aspects of the organization so that when they are asked to participate in the decision, they make a good decision. If they are only aware of their own little workspace, then they are not going to be able to make a good decision from a management perspective.

Despite the many good reasons for participatory decision making, new supervisors may find it hard to open up the decision-making process. Some new supervisors mistakenly believe that asking for help is a sign of weakness. "Get as much input as you can," asserts the director of a West Coast recreation department. "Two heads are better than one. Nine times out of ten, that is the case. Outside references are very important. You are not giving up any of your responsibility. In fact, you are encouraging your people to share in the responsibility of decision making. It is going to make you a stronger supervisor."

To those who think that it jeopardizes their leadership position, Marshall adds, "Don't be afraid to take input, and don't think that it is a threat to your authority. You have the authority by promotion. It is easy to be uncomfortable with that and to feel as though you have to exercise the authority to feel like you have it. Don't."

Hutchinson agrees. "If a supervisor does not use the combined resources of his subordinate and clerical staff, he is a loser. When people have had a role to play in the input to the decision, normally they will support it because they understand the pressures involved when the decision was made. They can see where they have played a role in that decision. You work as a team. You don't have one specific individual who is a dictator. Dictators don't last. Team leaders do."

Unfortunately, new supervisors sometimes think that they are using participatory decision making when they really are not. This occurs when they ask for input, but make a decision that appears to ignore the input. It is important to tell participants how the information is going to be used. "When you are going to make a unilateral decision, be participative, or merely obtain information from employees," says Fruchter, "you either tell them, 'I'm going to go with whatever you guys decide on,' or you tell them, 'I'm just going to try to take into account what you say, but this is a decision that I'm going to make.' [That way] they don't feel like you are getting input from them and then ignoring them; they know up front who is going to be the decision maker." And if you reach a different conclusion from the group's after having been honest about why you were seeking input, do not worry, says a planning and land use supervisor. "If you have good solid reasons, they may respect you more."

A third barrier that is sometimes encountered when advocating for group decision making is the argument that because supervisors have the ultimate responsibility for the credit or the blame for good or bad decisions, they should be the ones to make the final decision. If you think about it, however, the supervisor may choose the course of action, but the ultimate responsibility falls on the person implementing the plan. That person is usually the worker. "I have a thousand people that I am responsible for," claims an upper-level manager. "I have to be very attuned to the decisions that I am making and how they are going to affect the agents out in the field. The only one who is going to make that decision work is that subordinate. It won't be the manager, it will be the man or woman who is actually doing the work. Thus, they play a very important role in the operation and in my decision-making process." As a supervising transportation planner puts it rather succinctly, "You are not working in a vacuum."

Finally, group decision making must be used with some caution. Noted author Irving Janis (1982) warns us that some groups reach their decisions prematurely—without understanding what the real problem was, without due consideration of the alternatives and their consequences—because they do not want open debate to disrupt group cohesiveness. The Bay of Pigs invasion of Cuba and the Vietnam War are classic examples of "groupthink" in action. Presidential advisors discouraged effective decision making, and, as a result, the cabinet ignored obvious bad-decision danger signs (illusion of invulnerability, collective rationalizing), cut themselves off from dissenting opinions (via self-censorship and self-appointed mind guards), and viewed themselves as moral and opponents as evil (excessive negative stereotyping). A false sense of unanimity prevailed and bad decisions were made. The NGT and Delphi techniques are effective methods for preventing this premature concurrence-seeking tendency, especially if open inquiry is promoted. One way to encourage open discussion is to divide the group into two opposing sides to argue the pros and cons of any given issue. Another method is to hold "second chance" meetings after the decision is made to make sure that the original decision looks as good the next day after everyone has had a chance to sleep on it.

To Summarize

Decision making is one of the major requirements for being a supervisor. It is a skill that can be acquired and improves every time it is used. Rather than present a variety of decision-making models (operations research and linear programming, for example), we have opted to present in more detail a very basic model. The basic process consists of five steps: identifying the problem, exploring options and alternatives, picking the best solution, implementing the decision, and evaluating the consequences.

Each of these stages can be enhanced by involving input from others, both to improve the quality of the decision and to increase its acceptance by those most affected by it.

Granted, going through the steps of the problem-solving process, engaging in group decision-making methods, and encouraging participatory decision making is time-consuming (and there is precious little time in hectic public sector organizational life for the thorough and thoughtful analysis some problems require), but more time and energy will be wasted if the time is not taken. The advice of Mauro Garcia is rather pointed: "I would rather take more time and miss deadlines, than have something forced on people. In the long run, it will pay off."

Items for Reflection

1. Identifying and defining the problem is the first and most important step in the problem-solving model. Using the case example of the tardy worker, analyze the possible repercussions for defining the problem as one of the following: productivity, job satisfaction, adequacy of day care, legal liability, or fairness.

2. From your work experiences, identify a solution where you satisficed rather than searched for an optimal situation. Discuss and evaluate your reasons for suboptimalizing.

3. This chapter suggests that while the five-step model for problem solving can be applied to a variety of situations, the resultant decisions can be quite varied depending on the understood goal behind the problem itself. Describe a problem you are facing as a supervisor and discuss how the goals of least cost, shortest time, minimum inconvenience, fairness, justice, and equity might alter the alternatives considered and the decision that looks best.

4. You have just been told by your boss that because of budget cutbacks, your unit will have to increase its productivity by 10 percent. What difference would it make if you were to take a rational-comprehensive, incremental, or mixed-scan approach? Describe fully the effect of each approach on your decision.

5. With a group of fellow supervisors, workers, or students, brainstorm on ways to increase morale in the office. Use the Nominal Group Technique for reaching consensus.

4

Developing
Leadership Skills

Leadership skills are essential to the effective supervisor. Leadership affects the motivation and the performance of subordinates—both central concerns to supervisors. As leaders, supervisors communicate vision for their organizations and engage their subordinates in reaching that vision. To do so requires gaining the confidence of workers and developing ways to accomplish the goals of the organization. It also requires the support of *supervisors'* supervisors in pursuing the vision of the organization. If the work of the organization is to be accomplished, it will require supervisors at all levels who are good leaders.

Effective Leaders

What makes an effective leader occasions much debate. The literature on leadership first focused on traits effective leaders possess. Dissatisfaction with that approach led to examining the behaviors of successful leaders. The behavior-oriented literature led to characterizing leaders as oriented to people, process, or production, among others. Still other articles suggested that situations are important to leadership, and from that the contingency approach arose, in which it is believed that the situation creates leader behavior. For example, people would point to President George Bush and suggest that the Persian Gulf War provided him the opportunity to be viewed as a leader. Contemporary concerns with leadership suggest that in today's organizations, new demands are put on leaders (Denhardt, 1993). For example, leaders now are expected to involve subordinates in decisions and to empower them. Organizations themselves are constantly changing. The successful organization is characterized as a "learning organization" by some (Senge, 1990a, 1990b). The leader in the learning organization requires "the ability to build shared vision, to bring to the surface and challenge prevailing mental models, and to foster more systematic patterns of thinking" (Senge, 1990b, p. 9). The challenge is for the leader to foster the capacity of individuals in the organization to continue learning and developing.

Characteristics of Leaders

The supervisors in our study tended to agree that there are several characteristics good leaders share. Most commonly identified characteristics were a sense of vision, communication skills, interpersonal skills, listening ability and skills, and integrity. These characteristics tend to focus on behavioral aspects of leadership. They are reminiscent of, yet very different from, the old trait approach to leadership, in which all the possible traits of a good leader were identified. Today, good leaders need to be able to interact and share with their workers, so dynamics of leadership are more important than the traits themselves.

One of our supervisors suggests: "Articulate where it is you want to be. Recognize what it means. Get everyone on the same boat." This comment contains many elements important for leaders to create a shared vision for the organization. They need to foster understanding among members of the organization about where it is the organization should be moving. As Barbara Baker says, "leaders are able to capture [and] share a vision, and get employees to buy into it."

It is not enough to have a vision of the future. The current reality also must be understood. Then, a sense of "creative tension" between the current reality and the future creates the energy for moving toward the vision of the desired future (Senge, 1990a).

Leaders have to share power and empower others in the organization if they are to be successful in contemporary organizations. As Denhardt (1993) suggests, the leader must overcome the tendency to want to control and shed the aura of superiority in order to be successful.

Leaders who articulate a clear vision for their organizations are likely to have a coherent set of goals for their group to focus on and thus move toward, but they also are likely to be good communicators. As one supervisor put it, it is "most important to communicate effectively.

Expectations should be articulated clearly." And, "it is really important to talk to your staff; tell them where you're coming from." President Ronald Reagan was called "the great communicator" by many because he had the ability to express himself well in our media world. He was able to get people to believe in what he said even though most of his policies were not very popular with the public.

Interpersonal skills are closely related to the ability to communicate and listen. Tim Vasquez says, "Understand the staff as people rather than as part of a technical process. Each person is as different as a snowflake (as one author put it)." Another supervisor suggests "a good leader is somebody who is not aloof from the group." Clearly, people want leaders to interact with them as fellow human beings. The self-confidence and understanding that comes from easy interaction with others provides the basis on which to gain the confidence of others.

Listening is extremely important in a leader, according to many of the supervisors we interviewed. One supervisor sums it up for most: "Listening to your people and talking to them are the most important things I can think of." Not only do staff give their leaders good ideas, they develop respect for the leader who listens. As one supervisor puts it, "They need to listen. They need to always keep in mind that there is something that they can learn." Knowing what others are doing helps in deciding where to move the organization and helps to build trust in those who need to help in the process of moving the organization.

Not surprisingly, many supervisors identified integrity and ethics as important characteristics. In the public sector, issues of integrity and ethics are constantly in supervisors' consciousness because the public and the media incessantly probe the activities of government employees and attempt to find unethical behavior. The supervisors in this study often referred to honesty, frankness, and truthfulness as being essential for the successful leader. Because supervisors have discretion about when and how to act on issues in many instances, there are opportunities for misuse of their power. Temptations to help a friend or to use power for one's own benefit are always there. Successful supervisors resist those temptations and establish the understanding that decisions and actions are based on the best possible analysis of the particular situation and the mission of the organization.

Behaviors of Leaders

Research on the dynamics of leadership provides information on what action can be taken to move an organization to its desired vision. Theoretically, if we understand how leadership occurs, we can replicate it. Thus, research can be used to improve leadership, and supervisors can be trained in leadership skills.

Interactions between leaders and followers also are important to understanding leadership. One of the earliest authors on the relationship between the leader and subordinate was Chester Barnard, who believed that leadership depends mostly on the willingness of the subordinates to accept the legitimacy of the leader (Barnard, [1938] 1968; Scott, 1992). Thus, followers will follow only if they understand where they are going, if they are capable of following, and if the directive is consistent with their understanding of the goals of the organization and not contradictory to their views of what is right and wrong. Mary Parker Follett actually predated Barnard in many of these ideas, but it was only after Barnard's book was published that the ideas took hold. Follett believed that leadership depends upon community and that community requires understanding the individual members of the group and their interests (Follett, 1924, 1940). The emphasis on the follower's role in leadership moved the literature toward positive approaches to gaining the cooperation of subordinates rather than efforts to control through orders and sanctions (Guy, 1992).

Once the focus shifted to the followers, researchers attempted to demonstrate the most effective approaches to leading. As a result, a number of typologies of leadership developed. Tannenbaum and Schmidt (1958) developed a continuum of leadership behavior that suggests seven leadership patterns, ranging from boss-centered leadership at one extreme to subordinate-centered leadership at the other. The patterns relate to the varying use of authority by the manager and the areas of freedom for subordinates. The classic approach to leadership identifies three main styles: authoritarian, laissez-faire, and democratic (White and Lippitt, 1968). The authoritarian style is totally boss centered and leaves no room for discretion and input by subordinates. Control and coercion are the methods of supervision. The laissez-faire style is just the opposite, with no direction of any kind. The group is left to itself to function without direction or encouragement. In the democratic style, the leader is there to help and encourage. The democratic leader focuses on what needs to be accomplished, provides guidance in a very informal way, and uses positive reinforcement such as praise to encourage desired behaviors. In most studies, the democratic style seems to be most effective over the long run. While the authoritarian style may be effective in the short run, it usually leads to dissension and resistance over time. The laissez-faire approach seems to devolve into one of the other styles, depending on the personalities of the individuals.

The effectiveness of any leadership style seems to depend on two major factors: the personality of the leader and the situation, including the subordinates and their perspectives. Contingency theories of leadership focus on the dynamics in the relationships between these factors (Fiedler and Cherers, 1974). Thus, leadership depends on the leader matching his or her style to the actual situation. Leadership becomes relative, and no one style can be considered effective in all situations. Situational and contingency approaches to leadership focus on characteristics of the manager, the followers, and the organization as well as on the particular tasks to be performed. Each of these factors has an impact on the success of leaders. The effective leader, then, needs to understand the complexity of these factors and their interrelationships to develop an appropriate approach to fit both the overall situation and one-time (such as crises) situations.

Strategies of Leaders

The discussion above suggests that leaders must be able to evaluate their situation and understand themselves to be effective in leading the organization. New supervisors may find that a daunting task.

Strategies for leadership revolve around two major concerns—accomplishing the tasks of the organization and relating to the people who make up the organization. Obviously, the two are interrelated. In accomplishing the tasks of the organization, leaders must invoke the following of their subordinates and thus must relate to them. To relate to the subordinates, it is imperative to articulate the goals of the organization clearly. Because the organization's goals may not be the same as individual members' goals, the leader must act to gain consensus from subordinates. Finding ways to make organizational goals consistent with individual goals presents a major challenge with many payoffs in productivity if the leader is successful.

Leading by hard work and example seems to be a key to motivate followers. While subordinates understand that supervisors are not supposed to be just another worker, they also appreciate knowing that the supervisor is a hard worker and appreciates what workers have to do. One of the supervisors in our sample notes: "To be a good leader, you must first become a good follower. No matter how high you go in the chain of command, you must still report to someone above you. By being a good follower, you are displaying good leadership skills, because this sets an example to your people that you respect and follow the orders of your supervisor."

Being a good example helps immensely in establishing leadership. Supervisors in our study repeatedly focused on setting an example through such observations as:

"A good supervisor should provide a good role model for her people."

"Sometimes you have to get your hands dirty with the work you assign to your subordinates."

"Set examples and never be too proud to work in the same environment as your employees."

"Set examples and don't be a hypocrite."

Clearly, people like to know that leaders work by the same rules and expectations they have for subordinates.

Supervisors also suggested that leaders must take risks and empower their employees to take risks. Calculated risks allow opportunity for learning and for developing skills. As one supervisor says, "Leaders empower people to work creatively, are supportive of risk-taking and of failures—they allow people to try new things, and some will fail and learn by the failures." Allowing for failures is a difficult thing for supervisors to do because organizational life is so focused on getting things done. We often forget that one of the best learning devices is failing at something and learning from it. Effective supervisors understand that and work with their subordinates to help them learn from the failures as well as successes. Supervisors need to be supportive of their workers and stand behind them when mistakes are made. As long as the mistake is made in a good faith effort to do the work, supervisors must be supportive or risk-taking will never occur. Obviously, this does not mean that supervisors should be supportive of any mistake. Those resulting from lack of effort or misfeasance should not be tolerated.

Empowering subordinates also requires allowing them

to participate in what is taking place. Developing ownership of the work goes a long way in gaining commitment
to accomplishing it. Involving people in the processes of
managing and decision making generally leads to much
better efforts than trying to be the fount of all authority.
People understand the need for limits on what they can
do, but they also like to have some control over their own
activities. Those supervisors who recognize this quality
in people usually are much more effective than those who
do not. One supervisor notes: "Just because I have this
position does not mean that I have the market cornered
on brains." Workers tend to feel that the supervisor cares
about them as individuals if the supervisor talks with them
and demonstrates appreciation for how and what they are
doing. In addition to having supervisors seek them out
by walking around the work site, employees seem to appreciate having an open door policy as well. An open door
policy means that employees feel comfortable going to see
the supervisor. The supervisor who makes the open door
real is likely to gain the respect of employees.

Delegation helps empower people as well. Supervisors
need to realize that they cannot do everything. They are
supervisors to gain the cooperation of the other workers
in accomplishing the work of the organization. Thus, it
is imperative to be able to let go and delegate to employees.
Delegation leads to subordinates taking ownership of the
work and thus having a greater commitment to it. In delegating, it is important to make clear what is expected and
then give people the authority to do what is necessary.
People need freedom and discretion to be able to do what
is expected of them. Workers have a tendency to live up

to the expectations we have of them; thus, the effective supervisor has high expectations and allows subordinates maximum opportunity to meet them.

Supervisors who give credit to their subordinates also empower them. Being recognized for what they do provides reinforcement for employees. Without reinforcement that what they are doing is valuable, they may very well develop an uncaring attitude. Effective supervisors know how to recognize employees and do so publicly. As one of our supervisors put it, "Praise in public and criticize in private." Formal recognition and award programs have their place, but for day-to-day effectiveness, recognition and praise from the supervisor is essential and costs nothing.

The overall concern in interpersonal relations is for the supervisor to gain the trust of subordinates. That trust arises from all of the preceding suggestions. It also arises from treating subordinates with common courtesy and having respect for them as individual human beings. It comes from being consistent and standing by a decision once it is made yet being able to recognize, admit, and correct mistakes. Demanding respect seldom works; it must be earned. A comment by Lee Hultgren, director of transportation for the San Diego Association of Governments, puts these issues in good perspective:

> To me a supervisor's role is more process oriented. When members of my staff come to me with a problem, for example, generally they already know the answer to the problem and really want me to listen to them explain the problem and their solution and for me to agree with them. They are not really ask-

ing me to solve their problem because they have already solved it, they want my support. So, my role is to listen, to guide, to give them ideas, but I believe that most of the 'problems' that they have are problems to which they already know the answers. . . . I think the best way to supervise is to just spend a lot of time with the people who are working under you so that they can share their ideas with you and you share your ideas with them. It is a very informal kind of supervising. I've always done it that way, but I read in a book some time ago that they call it management by walking around.

Clearly, leadership requires some strategic actions by the supervisor, but the people who are supervised also are part of the process. Thus, leadership depends on the needs and desires of those supervised. The perception followers have of leaders affects the leaders' ability to lead. People must be predisposed to be led. Then they need to be given some reason to follow. The successful supervisor recognizes the immense differences among subordinates and attempts to develop strategies that encourage others to engage in the work of the organization. The next chapter deals more specifically with ways of motivating individuals to participate.

To Summarize

Leadership is a very important part of supervision. We have noted that the concept of leadership has changed over time. In contemporary organizations, leaders must have vision, interpersonal skills, effective communication and listening skills, and the highest integrity. The behavior of leaders and the strategies they use affect their success.

Peter Senge characterizes the contemporary organization as the learning organization (Senge, 1990a, 1990b). The learning organization constantly undergoes change. The effective leader is one who facilitates that change through the members of the organization. Senge suggests that roles of leaders are different in today's organization and include being the designer of the organization and its vision, a teacher, and a steward for the people and the organization they make up.

Leaders must encourage personal vision, foster communication, ask for support, continue building shared vision as an ongoing process, blend internal and external visions, and distinguish negative from positive visions (emphasizing what is positive for the organization and its goals). Successful organizations build on these activities, as the City of San Diego does in its managerial development program (Cleary and others, 1990).

Managerial effectiveness and organizational productivity depend on leadership to a great extent. Leaders who are successful recognize that those they lead have much to offer for the productivity of the organization (Guy, 1992). Leaders build on the strengths of those around them.

Items for Reflection

1. Identify someone you believe to be a good leader.
   - Describe the characteristics that make you think that person is a good leader.

97

- Identify the things this person does that are effective in leading others.
- List the elements of the situation that contribute to this person's leadership.

2. Assume you are a new supervisor promoted from the work group you are now supervising.
   - What can you do to become an effective leader?
   - What strategies will you develop in dealing with people who were your friends in the work group?

3. How are workers affected by a good leader? Why would workers do anything a good leader asks?

4. Interview a supervisor to determine important characteristics of a good leader. Then interview a worker with no supervisory responsibility and find out what the worker thinks is important in a supervisor who is an effective leader.

5. Do you believe that leadership style makes a difference? If so, how?

Building a Winning Team

Successful supervision requires working through others to achieve organizational goals and depends on cooperation of people in groups. To work through others, supervisors must build effective work groups or teams. There is nothing new about teams in the work environment. What is new is that teams are becoming the dominant way of accomplishing the work of the organization (Pearson, 1992). The primary work group is critical to the functioning of the organization. It is the focus for interaction between individuals and the organization and also serves as the primary social support system for workers. The employee's understanding of the organization begins with the primary work group.

Individual and Team Effort

Work groups normally have a particular task to accomplish, and most members of the group will be committed to co-operating in efforts to accomplish the task. However, we sometimes forget that there are factors that affect the ability and willingness of individual members to work together. Supervisors must be aware of these factors if they are to bring members together. Scholtes and his associates (1988) identify three major undercurrents in any organization that can affect team building: personal identity in the team, relationships among team members, and identity with the organization.

Individuals are concerned about how they fit into the organization and whether they really belong. Their integration into the organization will depend on their sense of belonging there. They consider who has influence and whether they have or are likely to have influence in the group. All individuals want to be listened to and be able to participate in meaningful ways. These factors affect their perceptions about whether they will be able to work with others in cooperative endeavors. Effective supervisors know how to make members feel a part of the group and draw them into the work and decisions of the team.

Relationships between and among team members are important to effective teamwork as well. Virtually all members of an organization want a work situation in which they can work together toward common goals. Conflict is a normal part of interpersonal relations. However, the human temperament is not always up to the task of coping with the stresses of the workplace. Supervisors need to work to make the work environment one where team members do not have to deal with conflict continually. Similarly, effort is required to ensure all individuals find

100

an appropriate level of comfort in the group. Otherwise, the group is not likely to work together.

Identity with the organization usually is assumed, but individuals may have conflicts between their loyalty to the organization and their loyalty to teams or co-workers. Supervisors and managers have a special responsibility in working to build team relationships across work group teams. These relationships help to bond the organization together and facilitate the linking of team goals to the goals of the organization as a whole.

McGregor (1960) suggests that effective work groups exhibit the following characteristics:

- The atmosphere tends to be informal and relaxed.
- Members understand and buy into the task of the group.
- Communication is open, with effective listening and expression of feelings and ideas.
- Discussion reveals disagreement and conflict but focuses on ideas and methods and not personalities.
- Self-examination is prevalent.
- Consensus rather than voting is used for decision making.
- Mutual trust is apparent—that is, each member feels that he or she will not be taken advantage of and thus can risk frank expression.
- Responsibilities for carrying out decisions are made clear and accepted.

The work group that reflects these characteristics is likely to function very effectively. The supervisor's challenge is to foster and encourage an environment in which these values and approaches flourish. Managing the human differences of the organization while allowing them to be exhibited sustains a high quality of activity. The supervisor needs leadership skills to manage these differences without personal judgment and with a focus on issues.

Functions of Teams

The basic function of the work group is to do the work of the organization, and that function can be divided further into subpurposes that facilitate the work. Problem solving is one of the major activities of teams. Problem solving involves maximum use of the knowledge, skills, abilities, and perspectives of each member of the group. Another function is to build a high level of commitment to carry out the decision of the group. Supervisors need to develop methods of accomplishing both of these functions if the organization's work is to be accomplished effectively.

Teams also help set goals and priorities for their part of the organization and contribute to the same at higher levels. There are various techniques for setting goals and priorities, but the team approach, with emphasis on individual team member participation in the process, is effective in gaining the commitment of individuals to the goals and priorities. Group participation usually also leads to greater specificity of goals and group norms supporting the goals.

Action plans tend to develop naturally from these decision-making processes. Deciding on action plans for implementation allows the team to allocate responsibility to individual members for carrying out particular activities. Typically, this process involves assigning different levels of responsibility, such as who is responsible for ensuring implementation, who has approval and veto authority, who provides support activity, and who must be kept informed of progress. By using the team process, the supervisor ensures that all members understand expectations of them and other members of the group. It provides an opportunity to examine and resolve potential conflicts regarding expectations and ensures common understanding of them.

Team approaches also permit examination of team procedures and processes—to identify what does and does not work. Dysfunctional procedures and processes can be discarded or changed and functional ones can be improved and supported through this approach. Team processes allow for examination of relationships among team members and can lead to efforts to resolve problems. In short, the team becomes involved in quality assessment through the entire process of work in the organization.

All of these functions of the team have the objective of improving the ability of the group to conduct its work. They lead to open communication and trust among individuals. The result is a climate in which problems are addressed and solved. That is the essence of team building. The key is commitment to the decisions of the group in all aspects of work activity.

Why Build Teams?

As noted above, team building is important to accomplishing the work of the organization, but it is important in overcoming conflict within and among groups. Interpersonal and intergroup conflict can undermine the effectiveness and health of the organization, although well-managed conflict also can be productive. Team building is one strategy for dealing with dysfunctional aspects of interpersonal and intergroup relations. Supervisors should recognize dysfunction through such symptoms as apathy of members, loss of productivity, confusion about responsibilities, lack of participation, conflict, lack of initiative, and complaints about service. If these types of symptoms appear in the work group, the supervisor should work on team building. Actually, team building is a continuous process that requires constant attention by supervisors.

Building Teams

Most supervisors find that the people they supervise do not necessarily behave as a team; rather, they tend to form small subgroups within the work group. These subgroups are the informal organization and are based on whatever commonalities individuals find to attract them to each other. Thus, those who have been with the organization for a long time or those who are new may tend to band together. Or subgroups may be based on similar interests outside the organization. Whatever the basis for informal organization, supervisors often have to find ways to bring the informal and formal aspects of the organization together as much as possible. Thus, supervisors need to develop team-building skills to motivate individuals to see a common interest in the organization as a whole. The process is not a simple one, but there are a number of small things the supervisor can do to build that common bond.

One important but often overlooked method of building team spirit is to be clear about where the individual and the work group fit into the whole organization. In other words, where and how does the work of the individual and the unit contribute to organizationwide goals. In clarifying the relationship to the organization or governmental unit as a whole, it is good to explain the constraints on the individual and subunit as well. By understanding both what is possible and what is not, the individual tends to have a better perspective on working in the unit.

Once workers know what the goals of the organization are and how their work unit fits into them, the supervisor should provide opportunities for them to participate in decisions about refining and accomplishing the goals. Participatory decision making is extremely important in building consensus on what should be done and how. As one of the supervisors in our study indicates, "Let the group spend time together to develop good communication skills that are effective to shared decision making." Another comments that "there must be shared goals and a shared desire to be part of the team." Shared goals come from participating in the decisions on those goals.

Participation in the decision making extends to asking workers to suggest ways to address problems. Suggestions should be strongly encouraged and then treated seriously. Employees will understand if a suggestion cannot be implemented as long as it is given serious consideration. However, they will not respond well if it is not considered and they do not get feedback on what became of the suggestion. Thus, it is important for supervisors to examine

SUPERVISION FOR SUCCESS IN GOVERNMENT

suggestions and to explain what is and is not being used from the suggestions and why. When the employees are encouraged to participate in suggesting how to accomplish the work and are treated as valued participants, communication in the organization will be healthy. Mauro Garcia explains, "An effective team is one whose members communicate openly with each other, are willing to challenge each other, are willing to disagree with each other, and are able to do this honestly." If the supervisor does not encourage open and honest communication throughout the unit, this type of healthy exchange will not occur. For the supervisor, it is important not to be defensive about criticism and suggestions, but to use them to make the team more effective.

Trust and respect are extremely important to effective teamwork. Effective supervisors facilitate the development of trust and respect. Open communication is important to a secure environment where trust can develop. When problems develop, it is important to address them openly with the focus on overcoming the problem rather than punishing those responsible for the problem. By addressing the issues openly and by supporting positive change, supervisors find workers and teams respond positively. They usually respond defensively to criticism and penalties. Defensiveness does not create trust and respect. Instead, it often hides conflict and blocks the flow of productive energy (Senge, 1990a).

Positive reinforcement is as important as identification and resolution of problems. The supervisors in our study frequently note that it is important to praise and give credit.

Supervisors who are open and generous with their praise of workers reap many benefits in increased commitment to the work of the unit. Recognition for contributions is a need of all people, and the supervisor who recognizes subordinates for their work builds teams. Supervisors should let workers know that they are appreciated. "Thank you" is easy to say and is very powerful.

Effective team building also includes worker participation in evaluating the work. They should be involved in deciding how to evaluate and what criteria to use. Shared goals and shared criteria for determining whether the goals are being accomplished lead to committed employees.

Supervisors have much responsibility in developing the type of atmosphere in which people can grow and feel part of what is taking place. Being strong enough to accept and foster open communication and to accept criticism and challenges to their ways of doing things is a must. Involving workers in the decisions and processes of the work leads them to buy into the work. They develop confidence in their own abilities to contribute and trust in the supervisor and colleagues.

The process of building a team involves several specific steps. The first step often is referred to as *unfreezing* (Guy, 1992), in which members of the group are brought together and made aware of the need for change or consensus is developed about the direction the team should take. Senge (1990a) notes that dialogue is especially important. In dialogue, team members suspend assumptions and engage in free exchange of information so that all can understand the range of issues and alternatives. The expectation is that members of the group can overcome defensiveness about their positions and perspectives. Once dialogue is successful, Senge argues members can engage in discussion. Discussion differs from dialogue in that members present different points of view and defend them. Unfreezing via dialogue and discussion together lead to consensus in the successful team-building exercise. Once consensus is developed, it is necessary to develop new procedures appropriate to the new consensus. Institutionalizing the new procedures is often referred to as *refreezing* (Guy, 1992). (The effective supervisor realizes that the organization must adapt to the ever-changing environment, so refreezing cannot be rigid.)

To ensure a team orientation, some team-building advocates suggest building incentives into the performance evaluation system. Specifically, team rewards such as pay increases based on team productivity may be a way of encouraging members to work as a team (Gabris, 1992).

These simple steps to building teams are based on values and assumptions used in formal team-building approaches. Organization Development (OD), Quality Circles (QC), and Total Quality Management (TQM) are some approaches used by consultants that include building teams in organizations. These and other efforts at changing organizations require in-depth analyses of the organization and complete involvement of individual members in developing goals and strategies for change. Supervisors usually do not have access to these approaches for continuous work with the work group, so it is important to distill the essential elements for keeping the work group focused. The major key seems to be involving workers in the decision-making process and treating individuals with respect for their contributions.

Effective teams result in high-level productivity and worker satisfaction. The organization with effective teams is one with a comfortable environment and a commitment to getting the work done. Teamwork requires continuous attention and practice in team-building processes. The team that pulls together harnesses energy, whereas the team that pulls apart wastes energy (Senge, 1990a).

Motivation Within Teams

What motivates employees to perform is the subject of constant debate. Each individual is motivated by something different. People are motivated by external rewards (extrinsic motivators) or by fulfillment of their psychological needs or drives (intrinsic motivators). Obviously, supervisors may have some control over external rewards but are limited in dealing with internal psychological needs. Nonetheless, supervisors are able to help create the conditions to motivate workers.

The three main theories of motivation are needs theory, expectancy theory, and equity theory.

Needs Theory. Effective supervisors recognize that workers have a variety of needs that must be dealt with individually. Contemporary approaches to motivation build upon satisfying what Maslow (1954) refers to as the hierarchy of needs: physiological needs, safety needs, social needs, ego needs and self-actualization needs, in that order:

- Physiological needs include food, clothing, and shelter. Work helps satisfy them through pay, job permanence, and acceptable working conditions.
- Safety needs are security, shelter, and absence of physical harm. Again, pay helps in purchasing things to provide for safety needs. Benefits packages of employers also help provide security.
- Social needs are affection, love, and acceptance. Informal groups help satisfy these needs, and effective supervisors can help make workers feel that they are important to the organization.
- Ego needs are those involving a sense of accomplishment, achievement, and self-worth. Status, recognition, and respect in the workplace help satisfy ego needs.
- Self-actualization refers to self-fulfillment or realization of one's full potential. Work can be part of satisfying this need through the opportunity to grow and develop increasing levels of responsibility and accomplishment.

As each level of need is satisfied for the individual, it no longer serves as a motivator. Each individual also has a different amount of each need and thus requires an individual approach.

Most organizations do not seem to build on needs as motivators but instead focus on what Herzberg (1966) calls *hygiene factors*. Hygiene factors refer to the physical surroundings, status, perquisites, and the like. To him real motivators are positive growth factors that build upon the intrinsic needs of individuals for achievement, recognition, and increased responsibility.

McGregor (1960) adapted the hierarchy of needs to the work organization and suggested the behavioral assumptions which offer foundations for motivation. He categorized work organizations and managers and supervisors as either Theory X or Theory Y depending upon the assumptions they used concerning human behavior and approaches to work. Theory X supervisors believe that most people do not like work and view it as a necessary evil. People are motivated by economic and security concerns and must be supervised closely to ensure that they are performing. They also attempt to avoid responsibility and are not very creative or innovative. Theory Y supervisors believe that people view work as a natural part of their being and enjoy the sense of accomplishment that comes from doing it well. People want control over their work and gladly seek and accept responsibility. People also have creative ability, which leads to innovative ways of accomplishing their work. For Theory Y supervisors, motivation comes from the achievement employees find in their work and from social acceptance and recognition. While contemporary supervisors realize that money and security are important, they know those things are only one aspect of what makes people want to work. Since the organization provides the economic incentive as a condition of employment, it is not much under the control of the supervisor, perhaps, except for increases in pay.

The supervisor has the most opportunity to work with the other types of needs of workers. They are the most difficult, nebulous needs, but supervisors can help make workers feel they are valuable contributors to the work of the organization. Supervisors can create the type of work atmosphere that fosters a feeling of acceptance and can encourage workers to achieve results, thus building ego and self-actualization satisfaction. These efforts usually lead to greater teamwork and productivity.

Expectancy Theory. In expectancy theory, motivation stems from an individual's expectation that a certain level of performance will result from a given input of effort. Subsequently, the individual anticipates some satisfaction or reward from the outcome (Vroom, 1964; Lawler, 1973). In order for the reward to motivate, it must be valued by the individual.

Effective supervisors use expectancy theory by making clear a direct connection between rewards and the subordinate's efforts. They find ways of providing just rewards and make those awards contingent on achieving goals. They facilitate the obtaining of rewards by clarifying exactly what it is the subordinate must do to obtain the valued reward (Pearson, 1992). Successful supervisors make clear what they expect and what subordinates, in turn, can expect will result from the effort they expend.

Equity Theory. For rewards to be effective in motivating employees, they must also be perceived as fair and equitable by the workers (Adams, 1965). People tend to compare themselves to others and expect that they will be treated equitably in relation to other people's rewards for given effort. If they perceive fair and equitable rewards when they compare their input and rewards to those of others, they are likely to be productive. If there is an imbalance, however, they are likely to become less motivated and less productive. An imbalance in either direction can cause dysfunctional behavior.

In addition to comparing themselves to others, people also develop standards for the relationship of input to reward in a more absolute sense. Thus, they have criteria for evaluating what level of reward they should receive because of their level of input irrespective of other people.

For the supervisor, equity theory suggests careful attention to relative rewards for subordinates. It is essential to communicate clearly how effort is rewarded and to be consistent across employees.

Techniques for Motivating

Numerous techniques are available to supervisors for using these perspectives on motivation. The most common one is to involve workers in the decisions of the organization. Participation in decisions leads to commitment and productivity. Although in public organizations there are limits to how much the work situation can be democratized, supervisors do have some discretion.

The meaning of employee participation often is very vague, and some efforts have been not much more than cosmetic so that employees begin to feel misled and manipulated. To be successful, supervisors must encourage employees to participate fully with the understanding that there are parameters. The important part is to make sure that employees have the opportunity to determine the methods for achieving the goals set for them and for refining the goals in the first place.

Allowing discretion over how the individual performs

the job also is important for motivating employees. Workers who control their work situation to the extent possible are likely to feel a stake in the outcome. Often, job enrichment or job enlargement are effective in stimulating productivity. *Job enrichment* refers to increasing the scope of the job by giving the workers more autonomy and broader responsibilities. Workers may assume a wider variety of responsibilities or may assume the responsibility for a complete service or activity rather than a small, specific aspect of it. *Job enlargement,* on the other hand, merely increases the number of activities without requiring new skills or levels of independence and responsibility. With expanding the scope of work and responsibility, there is less likelihood of boredom and lack of understanding of how the work relates to the whole organization's goals.

Many of these techniques rest on the assumptions of McGregor's Theory Y discussed earlier. Successful supervisors recognize that some people respond more to Theory X approaches. Most people, however, are likely to respond more to Theory Y, although everyone relates somewhat to both. Similarly, supervisors have styles made up of both.

Here are some simple suggestions for working with the diverse group of people likely to be in any work unit:

• Involve the people in the work unit in refining goals for the unit. As in team building, it is essential that individuals develop some stake in what is being done. Having employees buy into what is going on is a very effective tool in motivating them. To get them to buy in,

114

they must be part of the decision making process in the first place.

• Trust employees to do a good job. That trust means that supervisors should give as much discretion as possible and not constantly second-guess what the individual is doing. Rules and orders should be positive in nature and focus on facilitating the work rather than focusing on control of the behavior of the individual worker. Lee Hultgren says, "The most effective way of motivating employees is to give them a job that they enjoy doing and to give them the responsibility to get it done by themselves. Let them set their own schedules and deadlines. Let them set their own program." If employees feel that they are trusted to do a good job, they are likely to feel a responsibility for doing it and they also are likely to feel comfortable about asking for help when they need it. Trust in their ability to do a good job creates expectations for them, and most people do not want to fail in meeting those expectations. As Gregory Cantor says: "They are motivated by personal satisfaction and a sense of worth. There are no performance bonuses in the public sector."

• Motivate by example. One of the supervisors in our study says: "Show them there is no job too small or insignificant for you to do." While supervisors must avoid doing all the work themselves, it also is important to workers to feel that the supervisor is just as committed to the work as they are. Particularly important is that the supervisor be viewed as a hard worker who has as much commitment to the results as anyone else in the organization.

115

In order for any technique to be effective, it is important that communication be open and clear. Employees must understand expectations, the relation of effort to rewards, and the criteria used in evaluating performance. Successful supervisors keep employees informed.

The power of positive feedback should not be underestimated. As in team building, praise and recognition reap untold rewards in motivation. Bobbie Shaw, administrative analyst with the Office of Ethnic Affairs, San Diego State University, says "Motivate employees by praise; compliment and recognize contributions in meeting a particular goal." Charles Marshall goes further: "Use positive reinforcement as much as possible. Employees like to know that they are doing a good job. . . . There is nothing better to motivate employees than success. Put them in situations at first where you know that they will succeed." Robert Nelson feels very strongly that recognition is key: "When they do a good job, recognize them. When they do a bad job, recognize them. Just make sure you recognize them." The point is that people like to be appreciated, and they respond when they are. They respond when someone just recognizes that they are there, even when it is to recognize that improvement is necessary. People do not like to be ignored. By rewarding work that is done well and working positively with those who need help, supervisors make people feel that someone is paying attention to them and tend to respond positively.

Supervisors also need to keep in mind that individuals desire to be treated with respect. Open communication and acceptance of individual differences go a long way in developing mutual respect. As several of the supervisors in our study indicate, it is important to treat people the way you would like to be treated. As simple as that sounds, supervisors sometimes forget to do it.

Motivation may be a difficult issue theoretically, but effective supervisors find that common-sense approaches work well with most individuals in the organization.

To Summarize

Individuals participate as members of groups or teams to perform the work of the organization. The groups may be formally created by the organization or may develop informally as people associate with those they wish to.

Supervisors can affect individual and team effort through understanding and responding to what motivates individuals and groups. Good supervisors recognize that everyone is motivated by something different; thus, motivating employees requires many different approaches.

Teams help individuals understand what is expected of them and make work manageable. Supervisors can facilitate team efforts through clear communication of individual and team roles in the organization and by sharing decision-making responsibilities.

The modern supervisor recognizes that employees need to participate, be recognized, and be appreciated for their efforts and contributions. Participation, recognition, and appreciation are strong motivators.

Items for Reflection

Exercise I

1. Choose a group of five people and select a task or program activity all are familiar with.

117

2. Brainstorm about what the goal of the task or program is and how the goal is facilitated or hindered. Talk about all aspects of the task or program, with members of the group free to bring up anything they believe to be of concern.
3. Organize the thoughts and ideas that have emerged according to:
   • The goal or objective of the task or program
   • Strategies for achieving the goal or objective
   • Who has responsibility for each element of the strategies

Exercise II

In a small group, have each person write out what is most important personally about his or her job.

Have each person report orally on what he or she has written down.

As a group, develop strategies for incorporating these items into a system for motivating people to perform.

6

Getting Things Done: Influencing the Direction of Work

If supervision is working through others to get the job done, then it is no surprise that supervisory performance will be measured by what one's workers do. Influencing the direction of work to get the job done and improve productivity will not be easy. The notion that government can be run like a business (and its corollary, privatization), recurrent economic recessions, and fear of further tax reductions via referenda have caused public organizations to carefully examine their utilization of resources. Ironically, at the same time the public has questions about public sector efficiency and effectiveness, they also have very high expectations for service delivery. Failure to meet those expectations only contributes to the sagging confidence in public management. The net impact for front-line supervisors is that they are limited in staff size, in staff compensation, and in performance incentives.

Given these conditions, what methods can supervisors use that are effective, yet cost very little to implement? The responses to our survey suggest that there are two very divergent means to influencing the direction of work: direct and indirect. Although direct means of influencing work are traditional and do have their place, they are effective in a very narrow set of circumstances and should be used with caution. Whereas direct means of influencing work rely on hierarchical authority, indirect means involve leading by example and are more respectful of workers. Before exploring both means of influence, we will explain our bias toward indirect means.

Accountability

When a supervisor assigns a worker a discrete task or activity to complete, there are no automatic ways in which the worker suddenly assumes responsibility nor are there magical courses of action by which the supervisor holds the worker accountable. In fact, there appear to be limited opportunities for supervisory intervention.

To understand why, let us consider the work of Barnard ([1938] 1968). According to Barnard's *acceptance theory of authority,* managerial requests are not considered to be legitimate and authoritative until workers (1) understand the message, (2) determine that they have the capacity to perform the task, (3) decide the directive is consistent with their understanding of organizational goals, and (4) conclude that the directive is consistent with their own set of objectives. The point here is that the person making these decisions is the *worker*—not the supervisor. Until the worker believes that these conditions are met, the work does not get done—no matter how the supervisor may feel.

Does this mean that the worker is in control of the workplace and that the supervisor is powerless to get the worker to do anything? The acceptance theory of authority merely suggests that the supervisor must present directives in a very careful way in order for the subordinate to comply. In other words, the supervisor must clearly communicate the intent and purpose of the task along with specifics about what the final product should be. Note that the focus is not so much on delineating processes or procedures to be followed as it is on making clear what the goal is. Thus, an assignment to develop an on-site day-care center becomes clearer when it is understood that it is for all employees who are parents and not just single parents or low-income families, that the goal is to be self-sufficient rather than subsidized, that the facility is for healthy as opposed to ill children, that the capacity is to be fifteen and not fifty children, and that the purpose is to reduce worker stress and increase organizational loyalty.

The supervisor must not only reinforce but also increase the capability of workers to do current and future work assignments. It is unfortunate, but some supervisors believe that it is unnecessary to compliment workers— especially for just doing their jobs. It is not uncommon to hear "That's what you get paid for" and "Saying nice things will only go to their heads and they'll become lazier than they already are." However, not appreciating work and, more important, the person performing the work sends the message that there is no incentive for doing a good job. Lack of acknowledgment limits the willingness of workers to make a serious commitment to getting the job done. As for increasing the capacity of workers to take on more duties and responsibilities willingly, supervisors need to think more about who is filling the worker's position instead of what the position is on paper. By focusing on the job classification rather than on the person filling the position, supervisors miss the possibility that that person may have talents, skills, abilities, and knowledge that could be used to the advantage of the team. Thus, in the day-care center example, how well prepared the worker is affects whether the assignment is viewed as an overwhelming task, an opportunity to explore new horizons, an occasion to give vent to talents that otherwise might not be used, or a chance to reaffirm special skills.

The supervisor must convey a directive in terms of the worker's understanding of the mission—that is, the supervisor's request should coincide with the worker's understanding of the goals of the organization. Although supervisors may think that workers should obey all orders, workers are likely to refuse to engage in activities that run counter to established policies or are thought to violate laws or social norms (for example, falsifying reports or violating the chain of command). Further, the supervisor must convey the relative importance of the directive vis-à-vis other ongoing priorities or run the risk of the worker changing the priorities of the task. Thus, a supervisor can expect two very different responses to the request to develop a day-care center from an employee who believes that the organization's mission is to provide efficient services and from one who believes that the organization's goals cannot be accomplished until workers' needs are met first. The question is not so much one of picking the right worker for the job as it is of convincing the worker of the rightness of the job to be done. When there is mutual agreement, there is greater commitment to the accomplishment of work assignments.

Finally, supervisors must ensure that the completion of the task will promote the personal interests of the worker. Workers will put more effort into work if they know how the completion of work activities will benefit them. The gain need not be monetary. In fact, sometimes social rewards (praise, appreciation, acceptance, belonging, for example) may have greater and more long-lasting value. That is to say, the day-care project will be approached differently by a worker who is single and has never had children, than by one who needs day care, thinks that this project will lead to a promotion, believes that it is an interesting charge, or wants to do it because others would have a high regard for whoever made on-site day care a reality.

In each of these points that have been discussed, the supervisor has an opportunity to influence the direction of work. It is not a question of selling the assignment or of manipulating the worker into accepting an assignment that might later be regretted. Rather, it is an attempt to reach an understanding about work and its meaning. By reaching a consensus, both supervisor and worker empower each other instead of battling over who is in control.

What makes this perspective about supervision unique is that accountability is a two-way street. That is, in the final analysis, a supervisor cannot hold a worker accountable for a task until the supervisor is accountable to the worker.

That is what makes a seasoned supervisor view overseeing work differently than a new supervisor does. To be an effective leader—to work as a team—means that a supervisor must use subtle means of influence at crucial times. New supervisors think they have to make things happen—that the goals of the unit will not be accomplished unless there is constant intervention and pressure from management. Veterans realize that supervision really means that you must literally work through others to get the job done.

Direct Means

The supervisors we interviewed mentioned both direct and indirect strategies for influencing the direction of work. Direct methods involve face-to-face interactions between worker and supervisor, whereas indirect methods entail setting up systems to control various aspects of work. In the former, it is clear to the worker who is intervening. In the latter, workers are not interacting with a person but are responding to the requirements of the situation. As we delineate the specific methods, the differences will be more apparent.

In this section, we will describe several direct means of influencing work suggested by the supervisors we talked with. Be forewarned that a number of these direct approaches should be used with some degree of caution. Used improperly, the results can be disastrous.

Power

There is no question that a supervisor has the power to force compliance with orders. But as Margaret Mudd, a supervising probation officer, puts it, "Harsh direct orders may win you the battle, but lose you the war."

Power is very tricky. It is important that we understand what it is and how it is utilized effectively. One way to avoid problems with power is to recognize that there are many different ways to look at power. Kanter (1983) argues that the real tools of power are information, resources, and support. Because these assets are limited, whoever controls them can alter the level of conflict and cooperation in the organization. Wrong (1979) goes beyond Kanter's resource allocation model to discuss mobilization models, forms of power, and the dimensions of power.

The most widely known conceptualization of power is that of French and Raven (1968). They describe five bases of social power. *Legitimate power* is power that derives from the occupation of a recognized position to which others owe a certain degree of accommodation. That is, we recognize that a supervisor's job is to direct the activities of subordinates. Supervisors have legitimate power to order workers around. If the workers do not listen, the supervisor may choose to use threats—a form of *coercive power.* Or the supervisor may choose to use *reward power*—inducing performance through allocating economic and social rewards. If the supervisor is particularly knowledgeable, *expertise power,* the accumulation of a needed skill or knowledge, may be used to convince the worker to comply. Finally, some supervisors may be able to use *referent power*—that is, to get people to defer to them based on the fact that they are liked or because they have charisma.

From what has been described, it may seem as though the supervisor is all-powerful, but that is only wishful thinking. Supervisors rarely have exclusive rights to the five types of power. In addition, there are many caveats on their use. While supervisors can lay claim to legitimate power by virtue of their position, it is limited in many ways. A supervisor, for example, cannot make a worker in another unit obey orders. The scope of legitimate supervisory power is also circumscribed by the legitimate power of workers. In other words, a supervisor cannot order a subordinate to violate organizational policy, because the worker's position gives the worker power to refuse to engage in questionable behavior. Or, a subordinate whose job is to audit travel claims, for instance, may deny a supervisor's request for reimbursement for a variety of technical and procedural reasons. Further, legitimate supervisory power is restrained by employee rights that have been protected by statute, union contracts, and past precedents.

In similar fashion, coercive power is not possessed just by supervisors. While some supervisors believe that the only way to get worker cooperation is to threaten them with discipline, poor performance evaluations, withholding of organizational resources (pay raises, bonuses, training opportunities, secretarial help), or assignment to undesirable duties, coercive power tends to raise the level of conflict rather than bring it to a halt. In fact, workers can easily neutralize the supervisor's coercive power with their own threats, which leads us to a peculiar character-

126

istic of coercive power. Coercive power is very limited because it is more about making the threat believable than about actually carrying it out. What supervisor has not had second thoughts about following through on a threat when faced with workers all too willing to file grievances, spread rumors, cause dissension, organize a work slowdown, or consult a lawyer? Indeed, coercive power loses its power once one is forced to make good the threat.

Supervisory use of reward power in the form of raises, promotions, allocation of work load, recommendations for special assignments, permission to have plum vacation days off, and so on, are ways in which supervisors can induce cooperation from workers. However, there are other rewards in the workplace that supervisors do not control. In fact, supervisory rewards can easily be outmatched by worker-controlled social rewards. We all need to be accepted and to belong to a friendly group. Our identities, in fact, are often characterized by group affiliations (occupation, marital status, religion, ethnicity). Since workers spend more time with each other than with supervisors, worker-controlled groups have a considerable impact on worker conduct. Because we are social animals, being accepted into a society of other workers is far more important than winning perks and management acceptance. Not surprisingly, a number of studies have shown that workers will voluntarily hold back on production in order to gain the approval of fellow workers and avoid offending them. What worker would dare to test the ire and risk the ostracism of colleagues by violating social norms against socializing with management, for example? The price for doing so is too high and the social rewards for not doing so are too dear.

Expertise power can be equally problematic. Because the position of supervisor requires that supervisors work through others rather than do the job themselves, it is not surprising that the supervisor may not be the most knowledgeable person about a particular project or work process. In fact, the higher up the organization chart one climbs, the less one may know about day-to-day operations and specific procedures. True, supervisors may know more about the overall plans for the organization, but expertise power related to the worker's job is probably solidly in the hands of the worker. One interesting consequence of that observation is that the supervisor's lack of expertise power slowly erodes the foundation for legitimate power. That is, when a supervisor attempts to exercise legitimate power, there is a credibility gap. Workers are not likely to follow a leader whose competence is in question.

Referent power can be troublesome for a number of reasons. First, it is rather idiosyncratic, having less to do with the wielder of the power than with the inclinations of the subject of the power. Referent power is, after all, based on personal preferences known only to the person liking the other person. In our youth, for example, sports heroes, movie stars, and television personalities had referent power insofar as we allowed them to influence our ideas, attitudes, speech, eating habits, and dress. Second, while supervisors can attempt to increase their attractiveness to subordinates, it is not too difficult to surmise that given our decided societal preference for independence and autonomy, few workers are inclined to like their supervisor. Third, it is likely that referent power combines with worker-controlled reward power, and the worker's allegiance and loyalty are inextricable from group membership.

As stated earlier, power in any form must be used with caution. Workers tend to view force and the overuse of power as intimidation or manipulation rather than as friendly persuasion. How workers perceive the supervisor's means of influence, regardless of how it was intended, may engender cooperation or foster conflict. In the heat of battle, conflict can lead to surprising results. "Force, finger pointing, and demand are negative. When the court judge pointed his finger at me and said 'you *will* have new carpet in here by Monday,' I gave my notice," recalls one defiant supervisor.

Close Supervision

Close supervision is when the supervisor gives explicit instructions, monitors every action of the worker, and frequently intervenes to ensure the completion of assignments. It stands in sharp contrast to general supervision—when supervisors specify what should be accomplished but allow workers to use their own discretion regarding how it should be done.

Close supervision is frequently used by supervisors who think it is the way to take charge. However, it is really micromanaging, a process that a drug enforcement group leader equated to nagging. Rather than positively influencing the direction of work, close supervision has quite a different effect. "If you want to drill someone out of the

organization or bore them to tears," a large city personnel director contends, "just oversupervise them. That will
drive them nuts!" "If you watch a person too closely," remarks Samuel Oates, an assistant fire marshal, "you will
slow their growth" and retard their capacity to take responsibility for their own growth.

Several veteran supervisors thought that close supervision was caused by new supervisors not wanting to let go
of their old jobs. It was best summed up by Lee Hultgren:

> One of the things about being a supervisor is that
> you have to give up doing the work yourself. You
> can't do it yourself anymore. Your job is different. As
> a supervisor, you have to give up the job and turn
> that responsibility over to someone else. You are there
> to help them, to make sure the project gets done on
> time, to answer questions, and to resolve problems.
> But you are no longer doing the work. Some of the
> people who become new supervisors have a hard
> time letting go of the technical aspects of the work
> and assigning responsibility to other people.

Felipe Hernandez, a Marine Corps leader, agrees. "Don't
defeat the purpose by doing it yourself. Let them do their
work. Explain how something needs to be done, and let
them do it without watching over them. Oversupervision
is a morale killer."

Robert Hutchinson has his own theory about the cause
of close supervision. "New supervisors have a tendency
to overcontrol—perhaps out of their feeling of inadequacy,
their feeling of being thrust into a larger role, and in an

attempt to try to do well on a running start right out of the gate." But supervisors must fight those pressures. "Unless they ask for help," Ron Friedman, a principal planner, puts it, "don't interfere." "If you supervise too closely or help too much," says Cheryl Fruchter, "you actually create a worse employee than if you had given them a little leeway."

A number of other suggestions were offered to counteract the tendency toward close supervision. "One way," says an anonymous supervisor, "is for the supervisor to remember what it was like having a supervisor 'sit on your shoulder' watching every move you made versus one that gave you all the tools and left you alone to do your job." Empathize with your workers was the suggestion of another supervisor. Use the golden rule—supervise others as you would have them supervise you—argues a third.

"Bite the bullet," was another suggestion. "This is difficult, but it must be done. You must at times force yourself to give greater responsibility and freedom to your workers. You can't do it all. Many supervisors try, but they become overworked doing it their way. This results in their group not completing as much work as they are capable of doing. You might be surprised. Workers have a tendency to rise to a level of expectations."

Kevin Hardy gave very comprehensive advice:

> I think it is important that new supervisors do a couple of things right off the bat. Figure out what your organization is trying to do, figure out how they do it, and then try to determine, from whatever resources

131

they have available, how well the divisions working under them are capable of doing it. Review performance evaluations, talk to prior incumbents of that position (regarding problems, bright spots, et cetera). Then if you've done that, the only advice that you can really give to somebody is to believe in the human being working underneath you. Do I believe that this person working under me is a dummy, or do I believe that most human beings, given the opportunity, can do well? And given the tools to do well and the expectation to do well, that they will do well? I want to believe that people want to do well and that's where I have to start—from the presumption that people are good performers and that they want to do well for all kinds of different reasons. So it's important that you let them be themselves and establish their identity within the group before you start telling them how they can do their jobs differently, or how they might be a little more effective. You set a computer down before a person who doesn't want to learn anything about it and tell them that they'd be more productive. The fact of the matter is that if you've forced them to do it they probably won't be any more productive. They'd probably have a great computer sitting at their desk and never use it.

To effectively use general supervision requires knowing your people, say expert supervisors. "You had better know exactly what they are going to do," a large city personnel director cautions. "To the point that you can predict what they are going to do. If you leave them alone for two weeks, you had better know what they will probably do during that two-week time period. If you can't, then you have a problem as a manager. It's like leaving a bad kid home alone. If you don't know what he is going to do, you had better have someone watching him. So as a manager, you had better know your people."

One of the secrets to successful general supervision is to know the strengths and weaknesses of your people. "Some may actually lack the skills to perform one job," says a personnel analyst, "but could excel in another job within your workplace. As a supervisor, it is absolutely necessary to know these strengths and weaknesses. Find the best place for each employee to excel and feel worthy. Don't constantly harp on employees for their shortcomings. Try to find out what they are good at and put them in a position to do it."

Another method, one supervising administrative analyst tells us, "is to direct people differently. Some may require more direction, others more autonomy." It is a difficult balancing act, adds Fruchter. "I think somewhere in between telling someone everything to do and not ignoring them completely is where you need to be. Some people like a lot of feedback and some people don't want to be bothered."

Hardy asserts:

You've got to understand the human being. Spend some time learning about that human being, then try to develop a supervisory style that recognizes that humanness. Get to know your people and to understand that this is not just some subordinate. They've got a lot of needs and you must fill a certain role in their lives. Some people like a pat on the back, some like to be yelled at, and some like to be kicked in the rear end. People have different needs. You have to be able to address them and to have your supervisory style reflect that need for that individual person, because everybody's different.

Trust, of course, is a major ingredient in general supervision. "My advice," cautions one supervisor, "is to establish a level of trust between yourself and your subordinates. By reaching this level of trust, you do not have to closely supervise them and constantly look over their shoulders because you are assured that they will do the job correctly." "Believe in your people until they show they can't be trusted," advises another. If you do not allow "each employee the opportunity for freedom and creativity," warns an athletics director, "they will become disenchanted and feel smothered."

There is more to be gained by trusting than by not. "Trust and respect the capabilities of others," observes Tim Vasquez. "Even if they are each only 80 percent as productive as you. Four workers can produce 320 percent of what you can do by yourself."

Performance Appraisal

Evaluating the performance of subordinates is yet another direct method used by supervisors to influence the direc-

134

tion of work. Since the performance appraisal goes into the worker's permanent personnel record, supervisors can use the evaluation to motivate workers to meet or exceed performance criteria.

However, most organizations only require an annual performance review—an infrequent affair that may have some impact just before the evaluation, but little impact on worker performance for the rest of the year. Typically, because of the finality of the appraisal, neither worker nor supervisor views the process in a constructive manner. It seems that regardless of the validity of one's observations about worker performance, supervisors dread reopening old wounds (which seem to sting regardless of the number of superlatives that may have occurred in the rating period) for fear that the appraisal will have a very different effect than to motivate the worker to try harder next year. As was mentioned before about worker power, an upset worker's productivity may fall in retaliation for a less-than-satisfactory (and satisfaction here is defined solely by the worker) evaluation. Other demonstrations of worker power are also possible: the worker may flood the grapevine with juicy tales about the supervisor's "dirty laundry," an embarrassing grievance may be filed so that upper management questions the supervisor's capabilities, or the worker could name the supervisor in a multimillion-dollar harassment suit. Needless to say, both worker and supervisor approach these evaluations with considerable trepidation.

In spite of that, seasoned supervisors tend to view performance appraisal as a necessary tool that is underutilized.

Rather than the usual annual performance review, several veteran supervisors advocate *more frequent* appraisals. To them, evaluation time is not stressful because the purpose is not to criticize worker performance but to assess progress toward goals and to make needed modifications to the direction of work. Whether performance evaluations are seen in a helpful light hinges upon the supervisor's attitude. As Barbara Baker tells us, depending on how it is presented to workers, the reaction may be positive or negative. "It is a negative," she says, "when certain tasks are signed off by the supervisor. But it is positive for identifying where to redirect efforts, such as setting up short-term specific goals." One immigration supervisor describes the evaluation process as a thermometer—a way for both supervisor and worker to monitor progress.

In sharp contrast to annual reviews that leave no room for improvement except after the fact, frequent discussions of performance standards and expectations throughout the evaluation period can help workers monitor their own status, clarify the priority of duties, and, more importantly, modify activities to achieve a better performance before the critical final evaluation. In a way, according to Jon Torchia, "influencing people isn't necessary. Most people are eager to do this stuff and their training kicks in." In other words, approached the right way, frequent performance appraisals can be self-motivational. To facilitate the process, Baker suggests that new supervisors meet with staff bi-weekly for an hour. "Listen to what the employees are saying," she states. "Review with them exactly what they are doing. Set some areas that need monitoring. Don't expect that everyone is going to do the work the way that the predecessor did. The question should be: are *we* getting the job completed? Is it a good finished product?"

And if the work is not being completed, what then? Is it a case of "do-it-or-else" as one supervisor puts it? Although that is a choice that is readily available to the supervisor, veteran supervisors scrupulously avoid that type of confrontation. "It's easy to use negative discipline when they make a mistake instead of using positive discipline," says Charles Marshall. But "it is very important, especially for a first-level supervisor, to use whatever positive discipline is at their means to help maintain compliance with the rules and regulations of the organization. Write up people for good deeds in letters of commendation. Let them know they are doing well. Negative discipline is used as a last resort if everything else has failed." After all, adds a supervisor for a state lottery, "The job of a supervisor is not to be a watchdog, but to give positive reinforcement."

If discipline is inevitable, try this advice. "If you want someone to comply with something they don't want to comply with," says a recreation manager, "I think the best way is to explain to them why and explain the reasons why they have to do it this new way. That is always important. Sometimes you just have to show that it is the same for everybody. To make someone comply with orders and to give no explanation is about the worst thing you can do."

"If you must discipline," argues Mudd, "you have to have your facts. Be completely fair—be the same with every employee and without emotion. You can't get personal

137

with discipline. Be nonjudgmental. Finally, address problems right away and never close your eyes to what can become a serious problem."

If these words of advice are followed, then discipline should be no surprise. "If disciplinary action is necessary," says an assistant executive director, "it is something that should not come as a surprise to everyone. It should be well thought out and identified over a period of time."

Praise

Experienced supervisors told us that praise and recognition are essential tools in motivating employees. "The best motivator," a border patrol supervisor suggests, "is recognition. If they do a good job, recognize them. That motivates them. It keeps them going." That is why this particular supervisor instituted an employee-of-the-month program. In addition, he finds "the best thing is to get in front of the television camera and say that the men and women of your agency are doing fantastic work. That is the biggest motivator for them, when they get public recognition."

A labor relations manager recommends other forms of recognition: "Letters of commendation, genuine pats on the back in front of peers, giving that person increased responsibility, and expanding that person's individual ability to make decisions. I mean really delegate." Another suggests recognition in the form of attending training and temporary duty assignments. A third supervisor approves of electronic mail "to relay positive information to team members on a regular basis. Usually when one member does something positive, I let the entire team know, and I credit the team as well as the individual."

These supervisors downplay the role of monetary rewards as an inducement. One reason is practical: not only are resources limited, but personnel rules often restrict monetary incentives. In the mind of a public works director, "The only thing a public agency has to use as a motivator is praise. Unless they screw up really badly, they will get a known increase every year. Once you've reached the maximum step in a few years, there is no way to get any more money unless you are promoted." But a more important reason was expressed by a recreation department director. "In this particular field," he says, "you're not in it for the money. It is the concept of making a personal commitment because you want to do it. You see something positive—an inner feeling of self-satisfaction, bringing yourself to another level of competency."

And what about workers who appear to be just average? One supervisor thought it would be rough. But another, William McGuigan, was more upbeat. "Catch them doing something right," he says, "and acknowledge that in front of peers."

Indirect Means

Besides direct means for influencing the direction of work, there are a number of indirect methods. In this section, we will move from those means that border on direct contact with workers to those that involve the establishment of social systems that control interactions between workers as well as how work is perceived.

Good Instructions

One of the simplest ways to influence the direction of work is to give clear and concise directions. Supervisors are quick to blame subordinates when things do not turn out as planned, but senior supervisors also look carefully at themselves. "If there is a project that is crumbling," one supervisor points out, "it might mean that the supervisor is at fault." Perhaps the supervisor has not made clear the full scope of the project, the timeframe for completion, what needs to be done, or how it is to be done.

A supervisor warns, "The big thing is not to change your mind. Try to give clear direction." Says another, "Don't give a subordinate a task and then take away bits and pieces of it. It limits your credibility."

What is critical to giving effective instructions? A small town planning director says, "Communication is not you expressing, but others understanding." Another supervisor observes, "You have to make sure that there is no mis-communication—not hearing what you said, or not hearing you say it right—you have to verify that your directions are understood."

It begins with the supervisor having a vision, a mission, or a purpose. "To influence the direction of work," remarks Baker, "be very clear about the expectations. Understand and communicate the expectation for end-product results."

The supervisor must also articulate other expectations. "Plan the work, then work the plan," quips Hutchinson. "My experience," says a postal supervisor, "has been to

140

communicate first what the goals of the operation are, the time constraints or productivity factors we are working with, and to clearly define the tasks and responsibilities of each position. Communication is very important. You must state your expectations and your specific goals. With some employees, following up on the instructions is rarely needed; for others, it is almost mandatory. But regardless of the caliber of employee, as a supervisor, you should have complete knowledge of the operation or task so that you can understand how it works and where you should be at a certain point in time. It can save a supervisor some grief later down the line, when he has to explain to his supervisor that the employee did not know what he was supposed to do."

"With committed professionals," adds a highway mechanic supervisor, "I find one of the biggest things they don't like is having a supervisor who does not know what the job entails. Probably the best piece of advice I can give is to know in the first place what direction to go and what the job entails."

Giving clear instructions also serves another purpose. According to Ruth Ann Hageman, it is also a way of letting workers know that their work is important and that they have an important role to play. Put another way by a different supervisor: "The best way to have people comply with orders is to make sure they understand why they are needed."

Another thing that supervisors can do is involve workers in the setting of priorities. "For me," says a personnel supervisor in a small city, "it works well to sit down on a regular basis and say: 'Here are the priorities for me to-day. Is there anything I'm forgetting? Mine is not the be-all-end-all. Is there something you're working on that I'm not aware of?' I think that this works at all levels. It's a matter of sitting down and saying what needs to get done today, this week, this month. At all levels, this communication works to set the direction of work."

While the methods outlined here so far appear to be direct means of influencing the direction of work, they begin to cross over into indirect means in several different ways. First, the supervisor is relying on the structure of the task to organize the work, rather than using direct supervision. Thus, when the expectations have been understood, the supervisor does not have to constantly monitor the worker. The worker knows what to do and does not need additional supervision. Second, the supervisor is asking explicitly and implicitly for worker input. The workers are then committed to the accomplishment of goals that they value also. Third, there is a shift in emphasis from directing the people to directing the task. "Focus on the jobs or the tasks rather than the people," advises a supervisor with a quarter century of experience. "Present it to the employees in this way: 'We have to get this done.' Ask for help. Most people will respond in a positive manner. Ask for suggestions. This is positive for those who are self-motivated, and it tends to silence those who seem to always have something negative to say. Another way to ask is: 'If you were in my shoes, what would you do?' This is very effective in turning around those who constantly complain about things, but are never willing to suggest or give positive input to a situation."

Organizing Work

Supervisors regularly assign tasks and projects to subordinates. In governmental settings, as priorities shift and work loads inevitably increase, knowing who has what assignment and when each assignment is due can create problems. Veteran supervisors use a variety of methods for keeping track of work assignments, but they seem to agree that the method used should not require needless documentation nor should it appear as though the supervisor is "breathing down their backs," as one supervisor put it.

One method for organizing work involves keeping some form of suspense file, "tickler" system, or checklist. "Once I give an assignment with a due date," says a supervisor who tracks her work, "I'll stick it on my daily log so I know it is due that day—so I won't forget [after I assign it] it is due a week later, a month later, or two months later. I also have a tickler system in my drawer. I use Pendaflex folders and date each folder. There is a folder for each day of the month. When a certain project is due, I'll put a note in there and file it away for that day. That way when the day pops up, I can look in the folder and see what is due that day."

"My own personal style," says a transportation specialist, "is to make notes to myself in my daily planner. I use the planner as a reference for dates, phone numbers, and things to do. I also think it is important to keep up with the little things. If you don't, you will be inundated and they will get lost." Another supervisor uses a daily "to do" list. "I keep a list of things that need to be done, who's to do it, and when those things are due," she says. "I just check off things as they are accomplished."

Some form of a tracking system seems to be used by every experienced supervisor, but the secret to successful supervision is for the worker to have a system too. When workers adopt their own system of accountability, the supervisor can be assured that the job will get done on time.

A second method for keeping track of work is for supervisors to meet regularly with workers. Usually this is in the form of a regular staff meeting in which directions are clarified, priorities established, and problems solved. More recently, however, there has been a trend toward getting out of the supervisor's office and visiting workers in their environment. While a supervisor can, and should, keep track of work through regular staff meetings, there seems to be a growing preference for more frequent and less formal meetings. "A long time ago," a public works manager recalls, "I was given a piece of advice by someone I respected very much. He said that if there was ever an ironclad rule it is this: manage by walking around. It means that no matter how busy you are, take twenty to thirty minutes a day and walk around the office to find out how the guys are doing. This is guaranteed to make you totally aware of what is really going on, and it is something that data just can't do."

Another reason for walking around is that it increases personal contact in a potentially impersonal situation. "I keep track of work activities by being out there with the people and letting them know I care about what they are doing," says a labor relations specialist. "We have stats and all those kinds of things, which are really great, but nothing like walking around the workplace. Letting them know I care about them and my expectations that I have of them—that I don't think should be compromised."

A third method involves getting workers to report on progress—the filing of time sheets, daily logs, periodic reports, or a combination. Time sheets and daily logs, if coded by function, are useful analytic tools. They can provide both worker and supervisor with information about how time was spent. Monthly or quarterly reports are also valuable tools because they foster the evaluation of progress toward desired goals.

What distinguishes the way experienced supervisors use reporting methods is that they focus on measurable outcomes instead of on process. Rather than oversee every step of the process from beginning to end, seasoned supervisors tend to interact with workers when the assignment is initially made and when the finished product is finally turned in. What happens in between is recorded on the time sheets, daily logs, and periodic reports. That way, supervisors can determine progress but do not have to "breathe down the backs" of workers. "You have to check things," according to one supervisor, "but not everything."

Like other indirect methods of influencing work, the ones we have discussed are relatively unobtrusive. Supervisors are keeping a pulse on what is happening without interfering with worker autonomy.

Standard Operating Procedures (SOPs)

Using a procedures manual to direct work is quite different from directly supervising someone. "SOPs are a teddy bear," says Baker. "If employees get confused and feel awkward by asking, they can refer to the manual." "If you develop them properly," adds Kevin Hardy, "there should be very little else that you need to say. At that point, if they don't do what those rules say they are supposed to do, then there are rules about how you should approach that."

Veteran supervisors tend to use SOPs as a way to guide work activities. The idea behind them is to provide a means by which workers can answer their own questions about policies and procedures. In that way, workers become more self-sufficient and less dependent on the supervisor for constant supervision. "We have in the fire department a certain set of rules and regulations," says Marshall. "The rules and regulations are taught very early in each employee's career."

SOPs need not be rigid or unvarying. "Most organizations that I have worked with," a redevelopment director tells us, "don't have rules and regulations that are so onerous that it makes life terribly uncomfortable. I mean they are just basic—you get to work on time, you don't do drugs at work. They are just standard rules of work—not quite as strict as the military."

The real problem with procedures manuals is that they are probably out of date because no one has bothered to update them. While this is a project that a supervisor could do, it is also a nice assignment for a senior worker to assume. Writing SOPs is somewhat of an art form, but it can be learned, and it is invaluable in influencing the direction of work. Workers seem less likely to question what is written because they accept it as history rather than as a personal confrontation of their autonomy and discretion.

Participative Management

As we have hinted several times earlier in this chapter, involving workers in the decision-making process is a way to influence the direction of work without having to engage in close supervision. "Participative management is a good tool," Vasquez notes. "In asking staff to assist in devising a way to do something, they are sort of ordering themselves."

A building supervisor agrees. "I personally use the subtle approach. It doesn't mean that I haven't ever come to the point where I've let someone know that I am the decision maker, but I like the quiet approach. The subtle approach is more like sticking the carrot in front of the workers. People work harder if they are part of the decision-making process and help set up the goal. If I want somebody to do something, I ask the right questions and coach them the right way. It will be their idea and they won't have reservations about doing it. In this way, they buy into the goal."

Another supervisor suggests setting up employee advisory committees to advise management on various issues.

Being a Role Model

A very effective method for getting workers to perform at a high level or to follow certain policies is for the supervisor to set the example. "The most important piece of advice on influencing the direction of work of subordinates is for the supervisor to set a good example," argues a drug enforcement supervisor. "Model what you expect of others," says a school principal.

A third supervisor chimes in, "People learn how you yourself operate. They go by your actions more than by what you say. Do your best to maintain an appearance of being busy, work-oriented, motivated, and positive to instill this enthusiasm in employees." Adds another, "You walk the walk, talk the talk, you do as you say, you do as you expect others to do. A genuine, legitimate concern is the best influence in the world in terms of getting things done."

Workers are more likely to follow supervisors who set high standards for both workers and themselves. One way to lose influence is to set different standards for workers than for oneself.

Peer Pressure

J. D. Sandoval finds that competition among his staff is an effective way for them to police themselves. That is, higher performance is sometimes the result of natural competition in the workplace for organizational rewards, social status, or professional stature.

However, Hageman cautions that competition has its limits. "Cooperation, not competition, is what helps people work together," she says. "It is very difficult for a group that is competing with each other to work well together."

Although these supervisors disagree about the use of competition in the workplace, they illustrate how peer pressure can be used to foster a positive form of competition (in the first case) and a cooperative environment (in the second). Used effectively, peer pressure can reinforce organizational norms and standards. Although peer pressure in the right dosage and at the right time can lead to performance improvements and reduce the amount of

148

supervision needed, excessive peer pressure can result in the failure to recognize individual differences. In group decision-making situations, excessive conformity can lead to groupthink.

Office Space

The arrangement of furniture in the office can either encourage or discourage communication and cooperation. That is why troublemakers are often isolated away from others, and friends try to remain within earshot and eyesight of each other. Likewise, a secretary's desk is strategically located to control access to certain areas and people within the office.

In spite of organization policy, many workers decorate their desks to communicate social status and make statements. Workers on an open floor ("bullpen") have been known to demarcate their private territory.

Supervisors, of course, can affect what happens by simply altering the layout of the office. Seating arrangements that resemble a classroom, a theater, or a doctor's office are all designed to discourage communication, whereas most restaurant and conference-room seating arrangements facilitate discussion.

C. J. Lucke reports that workers in one office she knows about use different colored door hangers to control communication. A red door hanger indicates busy, yellow means caution, and green is a signal to go right in.

To Summarize

A common mistake that new supervisors make is to try to force subordinates; to mandate adherence to established rules and policies; and to dictate what is produced, how it is made, and when it is to be completed. When we asked veteran supervisors how they influenced the direction of work, they were, without question, adamantly against forced compliance. Yet, at the same time, it was obvious that they had not abdicated their responsibilities, either. An equally bad mistake is to have too few expectations about the quantity and quality of work. The only thing worse is to vacillate between a laissez-faire attitude and a dictatorial posture. Then workers do not know what to expect and begin focusing on the idiosyncracies of the manager rather than the purpose of the job.

In this chapter, we have presented both direct and indirect means of influencing work and discussed when they should be used. This chapter was not designed to be comprehensive, but to suggest some basic approaches that might be taken. It cannot be emphasized too much that the success of these techniques depends on proper analysis of the situation before taking action. Before doing anything, think. Think about what is to be accomplished in the long run and think about the consequences.

As Robert Hutchinson puts it, "The best advice is to sit down, observe, and keep one's mouth shut. We have two eyes, two ears, one mouth. Work it in that proportion: look and listen." Indeed, the secret to any successful effort to influence work is the ability to understand how workers interpret the meaning of that work.

Items for Reflection

1. You are ready to hand your secretary a letter for typing. You could hand it to her or put it in her in

basket, but you have just read about Barnard's acceptance theory of authority. How might you now approach your secretary in light of Barnard's four conditions?

2. French and Raven identify five bases of social power. Analyze your own social power. Describe your own bases of social power. Develop and defend a strategy for increasing your bases of power.

3. Pick one of the direct methods of influencing the direction of work. When is it appropriate to use that method?

4. Pick one of the indirect methods of influencing the direction of work. Evaluate its effectiveness.

7

Planning, Thinking, and Acting Strategically

Strategic planning focuses on the best fit of an organization with its environment through a clear vision of what the organization wants to accomplish, careful consideration of how to accomplish it, and agreement on responsibility for each of the steps along the way (Bryson and Roering, 1988). In many ways, strategic planning is a version of the rational comprehensive decision-making model with a time frame of five, ten, or more years. Usually, strategic planning is assumed to be the responsibility of top management, while the work units engage in short-range planning (also known as operational or program planning) to carry out the long-range goals. However, work units need to be tied into the decisions of top management, and the tools of strategic planning can be adapted to the work unit. At the work unit level, the processes might more appropriately be referred to as strategic management, strategic thinking, or strategic analysis, as they more clearly address decisions that affect the work unit's activities rather than the goals of the organization as a whole.

In the public sector, many reasons often are cited for difficulty in doing planning (McCaffery, 1989). These problems make strategic planning even more critical to public sector managers and supervisors. To accomplish such planning takes discipline, because attention naturally is focused on operations. It takes extra effort to think strategically about the future of the organization and work unit. To be effective, supervisors must be able to balance broad, long-term vision with the day-to-day operational details.

Planning is hampered by the time focus of many participants in decision making. Citizens usually look to immediate action and are not particularly concerned with what the strategies are for long-term enhancement of the community. Thus, work units need to focus on visible accomplishments that satisfy the citizen if they are not to be criticized as drains on the taxpayer. Elected officials also emphasize short-term activities. Because public servants are accountable to elected officials to some extent, when elected officials get into office by making promises of accomplishing something, they want to see results and the work units are the places to accomplish them. Because terms of elected office usually are short, the politician tends to look toward reelection and needs something to demonstrate having made an impact. Again, the administrators and their work units are the ones who must deliver. These short-term perspectives leave little time for long-range planning, especially when work forces are being reduced and asked to perform the same or higher levels of work. As one of the supervisors in our study indicates, "You don't have time; one day you are directed to do that and then the next day you are directed to do that. It happens a lot because you work for politicians, who are basically interested in short-term goals. They have to produce recognizable goals in a short term if they are going to be reelected."

Among supervisors we interviewed, the overwhelming response to questions about strategic planning was that supervisors do not have time to plan because they always are faced with more immediate problems than they can handle. Almost all felt that planning was desirable and important but unrealistic to achieve with any regularity. Repeatedly, they suggested that public administration is management by crisis and thus people react to continually changing situations. While proactive approaches would be desirable, they are impractical. As one said, "I find most of my job as a supervisor is to fight fires. Planning does not bring immediate results. It is a very intangible asset which cannot put dollars on the bottom line today. American organizations as a whole use the motto 'We'll cross that bridge when we come to it.'"

Supervisors also reported that strategic planning is difficult for them because they do not have access to all the tools they need. In particular, information may be lacking, and one supervisor suggests that power games involving control over information may make it difficult to plan effectively. In his words, "Supervisors possibly don't have the big picture. This is because a lot of people want to keep information as a form of power. Withholding this information doesn't do much for efficiency, but it maintains power." Clearly, this is dysfunctional. These kinds of concerns suggest that team building in the organization as a whole is needed so that such problems can be minimized.

The supervisors in our study recognized the value of planning even as they lamented the difficulty in finding time to do it. Following are some steps public sector supervisors can use in their work units. These draw on a number of works that suggest stages or steps take place in strategic management (Bryson and Roering, 1988; Halachmi, 1992; Mayo-Smith and Ruther, 1986; Pflaum and Delmont, 1988; and Nutt and Backoff, 1992). We are attempting to adapt a very complex theoretical approach to the situation of the supervisor faced with day-to-day challenges that limit options for planning.

Creating a Vision

As noted earlier, supervisors need to work with the group they supervise to create a vision for the unit. That vision needs to be tied into the overall mission of the organization. While the organizational mission often lacks specificity, the vision within the work unit ordinarily needs to be relatively specific. The vision includes a sense of what the organization will look like in some future time compared to where it is now. For the work unit, the vision is translated into goals and objectives. The vision, goals, and objectives should be simply and clearly stated to avoid any confusion about what they mean. Vision helps the unit to break away from thinking of things only

156

in terms of the old way and assuming that all change has to be incremental, building slowly on what exists currently.

Obviously, in the public sector the vision for the organization is framed in large part by external forces. The environment of the organization and the work unit provide many constraints for the work of the individual units within it. The work group normally has a particular problem or problems to deal with. As noted above, the immediacy of many of the issues and the expectations of results create barriers to vision. Nonetheless, the work group that engages in some discussion of where it is headed, where it is now, and how to get to its desired state, is likely to be more effective than one that does not. Work groups often have limited discretion in what problems they address, but they can prioritize them and attempt to address them in logical fashion. Thus, the process of envisioning goals can be used in examining what the unit faces and where to put resources. This examination includes analysis of the political realities, which affect the ability of the organization to do what it envisions. The important point is to involve workers in the process of creating a vision. One of the supervisors in our study notes: "Brainstorming with others improves the process. I have only one brain. . . . You're going to get a lot better ideas if you use more than one head."

Because the work group does operate within constraints imposed by the larger organization and the general external environment, part of its process of goal setting must include what strategic planners refer to as *environmental scanning.* Environmental scanning involves identifying relevant aspects and changes in the external and internal environment that affect the ability of the group to do its work. The relevant environment for the work group is the organization as a whole and the public with which it works. Thus, top-level managers, elected officials, interest groups, citizens, clients, and societal trends are part of the external environment. The internal environment includes resources and organizational culture, which dictate where the organization is going and what it can do.

Environmental scanning may employ many different techniques (Pflaum and Delmont, 1988). With each, the major thrust is to bring out the relevant information for making strategic decisions. Some type of group discussion or brainstorming is a commonly used approach. Supervisors might precede the discussion stage with what Nutt and Backoff (1992) refer to as *silent reflective techniques* in which people are asked to write down ideas or think about them before sharing. Eventually, free and open sharing of ideas about elements of the environment and how they affect the current situation as well as the future of the unit is necessary. The information sharing provides a basis for reaching consensus on who and what are important to the organization and what constraints and opportunities exist.

As Halachmi (1992, p. 554) indicates, the environmental scan involves several questions that should be addressed by the group:

- What issues, considerations, organizations, constraints, groups, or individuals should be included in the analysis and what should be left out?

- What is an adequate time frame?
- What is within the domain of the agency and what should be considered outside of it?
- What forces exist in the agency's immediate environment and what forces shape its environment by influencing the general environment?

Overall, the environmental scan addresses the stakeholders of the organization and what is important now and down the road.

Other approaches to environmental scanning include bringing outside experts together to discuss the current and changing situation and trends. Sometimes scenarios, role play, and simulation may be used as more formal approaches. Probably inappropriate for most supervisory situations are the Delphi Survey (Dalkey, 1967), focus groups, or computer simulation.

The environmental scan provides input to the decision-making process for the work group. It also provides a sense of what the future is likely to bring. Decisions on goals and objectives must be tempered both by what exists now and by what the future is expected to be. It does little good to develop goals and objectives toward an ideal if there is no realistic possibility of having the support or other resources to accomplish them. The effective supervisor is able to identify the resources and constraints affecting the group and to project them into the future as part of the information workers use in making team decisions.

In contemporary public administration, much attention is paid to envisioning quality or excellence as part of the goals and objectives of the work. The Total Quality Management movement prominent in public sector discussions these days focuses on quality as a primary goal of every part of the organization. Quality service to the customer, whether internal or external to the work group, is viewed as the ultimate goal. By focusing on quality (sometimes referred to as zero defects) at every step of the work process, workers avoid mistakes or correct them immediately to avoid compounding the error. If errors are corrected on the spot, time and money are saved by not having to go back later and correct entire products or services.

At the same time, flexibility is imperative in the public sector. Because of the changing direction of policy decisions from the public and elected officials, public sector supervisors must always be ready to adapt to the new directions.

Clearly, the supervisor must understand the organizational mission and be able to communicate it to the workers. Helping the workers to then develop a vision for the work unit consistent with the mission of the organization is a major challenge facing the supervisor. Part of that process includes refining the mission of the organization to make it meaningful relative to the work unit itself. Of course, communication of issues and difficulties faced by the work unit to the higher levels of management is also important for the supervisor. Keeping the vision alive is a continuous process.

Setting Goals

In the second stage of strategic management, the group decides what it wishes to do. It uses the information from

its environmental scan along with preferences of participants to decide what it wants to do and what it can do.
This phase often is called *strategic analysis* and results
in establishment of priorities. Numerous techniques exist
for prioritizing, but most supervisors will find that rank-
ing of goals by participants with open discussion usually
results in consensus.

Devising Plans of Action

Once goals are established, it is necessary to devise action plans for accomplishing them. All too often, supervisors and managers assume that decisions will be implemented automatically. The successful supervisor knows
that the process requires careful design of action plans.
The effective supervisor involves the work-group members in the process as much as possible. The ideal approach
is to identify and consider all alternatives for achieving the
desired results. Such an ideal approach normally is unrealistic because there are many constraints to identifying and
considering all alternatives. Time constraints, as discussed,
are especially important in the public sector. Resources
are likely to be limited. The knowledge and abilities of
the participants in the decision-making process limit the
alternatives that may be considered. The information available to participants also tends to be limited. The result is
decisions made on the basis of bounded rationality, meaning that the organization has limited capacities to consider
all aspects of any potential decision. The constraints to
identification and consideration of alternatives may be
viewed as boundaries.

161

Choosing Strategies

Consideration of alternative strategies requires assessment of the resources available to apply to the situation at hand. Thus, part of the decision-making process is considering what resources are needed for any given strategy and how they compare with what is available. The supervisor needs to keep the group informed about realistic expectations of resources, yet should not just be a naysayer undermining any creative ideas because they have costs associated with them. Flexibility in adjusting to changing conditions in the environment is as important here as in goal setting. As much as possible, changing environmental conditions should be anticipated, but resources need to be available should the unexpected appear. Planning for the unexpected sounds like an oxymoron, but real life work requires it to some extent.

The analysis of alternative strategies focuses on results as well as costs. Some form of cost-benefit analysis is appropriate for such choices, although it is unlikely that a formal cost-benefit analysis will take place in most work groups. By considering the likely outcome of any strategy and what it will require in resources, the discussion actually focuses on benefits received for given cost. Supervisors generally will not apply a complex formula to this consideration, but workers usually have some sense of what inputs, outputs, and outcomes are likely to be.

One of the key assessments in the public sector is what political effect any action is likely to have. Elected officials are very sensitive to anything that is likely to be controversial, and outside groups (especially the media) are very attentive. Thus, in developing strategies, supervisors and their work groups have to be sensitive to the reality of the fishbowl existence of public agencies. Political feasibility often is just as important as technical feasibility in deciding on strategic alternatives.

Formulating an Implementation Plan

After assessing strengths and weaknesses of alternative strategies, a choice is made and then responsibility must be parceled out to accomplish the goals and objectives. The implementation plan focuses on specific objectives to be accomplished within a specified time period. Outcome or performance indicators are identified and responsibility for their achievement is assigned. These processes assure that the plan is given real life by being linked with the activities of the work unit. As in all other phases of planning, participation of the workers responsible for performance is essential to effective results. Sharing of information on a regular basis facilitates achievement of goals.

Implementation plans also provide for monitoring the progress toward the goal. There are numerous levels of monitoring, including the group assessment of progress. Usually, the supervisor assumes a large part of the monitoring function. However, individual employees with specific responsibilities do some self-monitoring, and their interactions with other members of the group provide opportunity for mutual monitoring. Establishment of milestones provides a tangible measure for monitoring and evaluation. The supervisor should also work with the group in developing regular discussion of how well it is doing. This type of interaction also serves as a motivator of individual group members through peer pressure.

Monitoring is an important part of the process that includes analyzing changes or results brought about by the plan and its implementation. Monitoring requires setting up an evaluation process, which determines whether things are going as planned. It also provides for continuity and specificity in accomplishment of goals. Monitoring results in constant assessment of the plan as well as the assumptions and values on which the plan is based. As elements of the environment and the organizational culture change, monitoring helps to keep the unit current.

Strategic management is a process that requires continuous action to maintain. It requires discipline on the part of the supervisor to put aside time for planning on a regular basis and to keep work-group members involved in the process. As Nutt and Backoff (1992, p. 164) say, the strategic manager must "be a facilitator, teacher, and politician as well as a technician."

To Summarize

Strategic planning helps organizations focus on what they would like to be doing in the future. Strategic management focuses on the work unit and its fit within the overall plan. Strategic management requires creating a vision consistent with the organization's mission, understanding the environment in which the organization operates, setting goals, and then devising actions to implement the plan. Supervisors must involve employees in each step of the planning process to ensure success.

Items for Reflection

1. You are part of the strategic management task force of the police department. What are the relevant elements of the environment the task force should consider in developing a strategic plan?
2. How would you involve individual employees in the strategic planning process in your organization?
3. As part of a group, discuss obstacles to long-range planning and consider how such obstacles could be overcome.

Part Three

PROBLEM SOLVING
FOR SUPERVISORS
IN GOVERNMENT

8

Dealing with Politics and Politicians

Politics in the workplace is a difficult issue for supervisors to deal with—whether it is external politics, such as an elected official trying to tell public servants how to do their jobs, or internal office politics, such as people in the office forming factions to do mortal battle with each other. Supervision—working through others to accomplish organizational goals—is demanding enough without having to account for the intrigue and the power struggles that tend to accompany both forms of politics. Yet politics is an inescapable part of public sector work.

Internal office politics is particularly troublesome for new supervisors—especially those who are unsure of their role and power; have tenuous relationships with superiors, fellow supervisors, and subordinates; or are not well-read on organizational history. From an interpersonal perspective, rapidly shifting political winds and a multitude of hidden agendas can make the typical supervisor leery of purported friendships and mutual-benefit alliances. If the political environment of the organization is too entangled, ultimately, teamwork and cooperation may be the price that is paid for the suspicion brought about by political dynamics.

A sense of frustration and exasperation is often expressed when the topic of external politics is brought up. External political pressure plays havoc with supervisors' ability to take carefully measured steps to maintain a cooperative and harmonious workplace. It often forces supervisors to weigh rational choices against seemingly irrational ones; to consider sacrificing long-term goals for the sake of dubious short-term strategies and short-lived efficiencies; to pit loyalty to the organization against allegiance to vocal and influential special interest groups; to ponder the consequences of advocating the good of the group at the expense of personal survival. In a highly charged political environment, trying to get access to accurate information for decision-making purposes may be futile as various factions muddy the water by spreading disinformation and supercharging the emotional atmosphere with rumors.

It is understandable that the first inclination of many supervisors is simply to avoid anything that might resemble politics. However, avoiding internal or external politics is virtually impossible, since appointment to the position of supervisor axiomatically makes one a part of the political scene. Because a supervisor's job involves making decisions, it should be no surprise that every super-

visory decision has some political repercussion both inside and outside the workplace.

As the supervisor becomes aware of the stakes, the possible consequences of a bad political decision begin to bear
heavily on the decision-making process. However, to hesitate or to choose not to decide can be as dangerous as making a political decision hastily with too little information.
In a highly charged political situation, one false move could
mean standing in line at the unemployment office. As the
director of a major state organization once said, "You enter
the position with a bag full of chips. You play them as
needed. You win some and you lose some. But when they
are all gone, the game is over."

Although this chapter will increase the reader's understanding of both forms of politics, there is no easy way
to deal with them. In fact, interestingly (and rather ironically), making the right choice and solving a difficult problem seldom leads to a permanent cure. Political power is
quite ethereal. More often than not, making the right political decision only means that the game will continue and
players can face yet another round of even more knotty
choices.

Be that as it may, the message here is that when it comes
to politics, it is not a question of whether or not to play,
but of *how* to play for as long as one can.

Am I a Politician or a Supervisor?

At some point in time, new supervisors ask themselves the
question: "Am I a politician or a supervisor?" This is usually
when they are embroiled in a sticky political situation

where all sight of organizational goals is lost. The desire is to remain neutral and goal-oriented, but the reality is that the organization's objectives cannot be achieved unless one has the political clout to alter internal organizational processes and to influence the external political agenda. To gain that power, one must play politics.

It is not always a comforting feeling, but a supervisor's personal survival depends on political savvy. At times one feels as though one has been coerced into political entanglements and perhaps been made to act in an unprofessional manner. Not surprisingly, some supervisors feel that they have betrayed themselves, their profession, their organization, and their workers by resorting to morally questionable methods. Even when the ends may justify the means, the degree of rationalizing and mental gymnastics that must be engaged in are disquieting for the average supervisor.

The reason new supervisors know so little about politics is that frontline workers are promoted into supervisory positions because they are top producers who pay attention to achieving organizational goals. Being focused on attaining goals rather than playing politics is probably one of the major reasons they are promoted. Think about it: what manager would hire a supervisor who was too good at scheming and plotting? It might cost that manager his or her job.

The natural reaction is to be somewhat offended by politics, but the dynamics of power in organizational life cannot be ignored. To have a more enlightened view of politics, we must first understand that supervisors are engaged in politics and political decisions on an ongoing basis, whether they think they are or not. For example, let us say that several subordinates ask for the same Thanksgiving weekend off. If the supervisor grants all the requests, there will be inadequate office coverage. Is the question of who goes and who stays a political decision or a matter of applying the appropriate policy?

If we look more closely at the situation, it is obvious that regardless of the actual policy, the typical supervisor must weigh many factors: who asked first, who has seniority, who had the last four-day weekend, who has asked for upcoming holiday weekends, who has relatives coming into town, who has been particularly productive and deserving of time off, and so on. As the supervisor interprets the policy in light of these factors, a variety of personal judgments about what is good for the organization are being made. That involves politics, whether the motive is for the good of the whole (for example, treating everyone equally by rotating four-day weekends regardless of special circumstances such as hardship) or for the good of a few (for example, rewarding those who have made the greatest contribution regardless of the last time they had a long weekend off). As the supervisor gathers information from each of the competing workers, elements of politics will be present. Politics can be subtle. Who the supervisor asks to respond to certain questions and what questions are asked can be interpreted as forms of pressure. In the final analysis, the decision about the vacation schedule is a political statement that sends a clear message about "allies" and "enemies." Those who "won" feel that their power is reinforced, and those who "lost" will likely attempt to forge a coalition with other dissident forces. This political assessment of the supervisor's decision will occur no matter how vehemently the supervisor denies that politics were involved.

What this example shows is that personal preferences, or politics, are an integral part of any supervisory decision. And since supervisors make many decisions, they are automatically involved in politics. As Kevin Hardy defines it: "How you interact with different people, what types of interests you are trying to promote, and the agenda you are pursuing, all represent, in one definition or another, what politics is."

Politics also involves understanding your workers' special interests. Hardy goes on to say, "You need to understand what your subordinates need. You have to have an understanding of what it is that they want to get out of their time with you. People bring all kinds of different interests to work—whether to make more money, to gain prestige, or to get job security. Essentially, you have to be able to take those interests, focus them towards your work objectives, and try to make them a positive force." That is, politics easily becomes a factor in supervisory decision making because few questions are matters of pure fact where rationality prevails. Instead, most decisions involve preferences for certain values—whether siding with the organization's goals; with the worker's wants; or with a superordinate value, such as justice, fairness, or equity. In the end, by making a decision—even favoring what workers want—supervisors are stating a preference and using their power to defend that preference.

It Is Unavoidable

Though politics and politicians may cause the average supervisor many headaches, as aspects of the workplace they cannot be overlooked. "If you choose to ignore it," says Hardy, "you are going to get burned again and again. A lot of people do choose to ignore it and those people are left behind because it is an integral part of bringing human beings together. You can't avoid politics."

According to Cheryl Fruchter, "If you ignore it, you could have a great idea slammed down because you make little errors in strategy rather than because it's a bad idea. So I think it's naive not to take it into account."

Of course, that does not mean that one has to like it. "Some people really thrive on it," Fruchter continues, "but I think most don't enjoy it. Most in an ideal world would just do the best they could. But that's just not the way reality is. So I think you have to accept it and try to work around it."

A public works manager agrees: "Look at the reality of the situation. There really is no way to overcome politics. Don't expect to overcome it, because you won't. You do have to be aware of it—taking into account who is buddy-buddy. But it can't be eliminated."

Supervisors' advice on how to cope with politics fell into two categories: dealing with politicians and handling office politics. But first, to help the new supervisor understand why politicians are sometimes a problem, let us examine some specific concerns.

Problems with Politicians

To the average supervisor, politicians are a blessing and a curse. When policies and practices coincide, things could not be any better between supervisor and politician. But when there are differences of opinion about what to do, when to do it, or how to do it, a number of complaints are heard from supervisors.

Micromanagement

While most public servants would not presume to tell elected officials how to conduct business (for instance, running a political campaign), some elected officials and their staffs seem to feel that government organizations work for them and ought to follow their direction. When politicians try to direct the activities of public agencies, there can be hard feelings.

Supervisors get upset with politicians who meddle with operations. "I feel politicians micromanage when they should macromanage," an associate athletics director observes. "They try to interfere with minute details when they are not qualified to." A recreation manager agrees, "Oftentimes politicians don't realize fully the department's functions—they're not clear about what you do, the priorities within the department, and how it really works."

Gregory Cantor gives an example:

176

Some residents complained about speeders in their neighborhood. The city council complained to the chief. The chief went to the captains; the captains to the sergeants. The result was a command to use radar to enforce the limit strictly—even citing people one or two miles over the limit. However, when radar is used, an engineering study must be done first to determine how many people follow the speed limit. To allow radar use, 80 to 85 percent of the cars must normally travel within five miles per hour over the speed limit. If it is less than that, it is determined that the posted speed is too low—a speed trap. The end result was that we couldn't enforce the speed limit with radar unless we raised the limit. We couldn't raise the limit as this was a residential street—so no enforcement could be done.

"I think too often politicians don't realize what operations are," adds a personnel manager in a major city. "They have so much to do. When we tell them something—'We can do this program and this is how much it's going to cost'—it took us months to come up with the program. We spend about three minutes briefing them and asking them to go along with it. There is a general lack of appreciation."

However, the lack of appreciation may go both ways. He continues, "We don't appreciate all the work they have to do, and they don't appreciate (probably because they find it boring) all the operations stuff. I don't think there is any like or dislike—I think it is a matter of neither side

177

caring about the other's problems. That creates problems when they judge one another's turf."

The politician's "turf," of course, is responsiveness to constituents. Constituent complaints can be the source of many problems for government workers. "Very often," a federal employee tells us, "politicians react to, and expect action on, complaints from the public that are unsubstantiated and time-consuming to respond to." "They may make promises that they feel should be taken care of," says Mauro Garcia. "That puts an extra burden on the staff. Projects might have to be shuffled to meet public deadlines set by politicians. This shuffling might cause a needed project to be put on hold."

A government worker's priorities are different from a politician's. An experienced supervisor explains it this way. "The manager's position is that we want the service distributed as equitably as possible, so we put things on a priority list. If it is a public safety item, that is the 'A' priority. If someone is going to get hurt, we do that first—that's an emergency, whereas the politician's priority is that the citizen is giving him a hard time. It may be a campaign supporter or just a strong community leader. It's not an emergency, but that's the important one. So that's where you get a clash of differences."

Direct Orders

Politicians and their staffs sometimes get carried away with their power and try to direct the activities of individual workers without going through the organizational hierarchy. Says Robert Nelson:

The biggest problem is the individual politician who doesn't recognize his role. As a member of a board or legislative body, he has one vote. He shouldn't give a direct order to someone in the field. An example of that comes to mind: in a city that I worked for, a city councilperson came down to a crime scene in progress. The councilperson walked right up to the sergeant and started to order the sergeant to do something in relation to this crime scene. The sergeant arrested the councilmember and removed the councilperson from the scene. It was clear that the officer knew who was in charge and what his own role was.

This confusion of roles is particularly troublesome during election time. A management analyst gives the following advice:

You have to be very careful, because city councilmembers all ask for staff assistance. You're in the awkward position of determining whether it is normal staff assistance or if they are really trying to get you to help on their campaign, which is not legal or ethical. It's very awkward for staff to have to tell a councilperson that they can't do what they were told to do. The mayor comes in the office and says, "I want you to do this." And you've been told not to do anything for the mayor. So you have to say that you will check with your boss. Then, very often in a situation like this, your boss says, "Oh, well, she should have just done it." You have your higher-ups playing to them, too. So it can put you in a very awkward situation. It is something that you just kind of grin and bear. If you make a mistake in dealing with elected officials and give them something you shouldn't have, or not give them something you're supposed to, that's when people get really touchy.

Changes in Policy

Supervisors also get upset with politicians when there are sudden shifts in policy. Public servants can work for months on a project only to find that it is no longer a priority with the city council. Or, seemingly out of the blue, the board of supervisors will mandate that a project be expedited— upsetting existing priorities and putting current projects on the back burner. Or, as the result of elections, existing policies are reversed.

"They want to give direction that changes from day to day," observes Leroy Brady. This can be rather disconcerting because "the business side of supervision needs a plan they can stick with. Politicians listen to public sentiment and let that influence the decisions they will make. Being in the public's eye is what the politician wants, while the organization just wants to complete its goal."

A school superintendent shares an example of how suddenly political shifts can occur: "In my case, I deal with the school board, which is elected to serve the public. They are mandated to do what's best for education. The boards are often influenced by vocal minorities, and individual interest groups become too involved. The administration wrote a resolution and gave it to the board to see if the resolution expressed the board's policy." But rather than

180

edit the resolution for conformity to the policy, the board instead rewrote the entire policy.

"The lack of predictability of politicians," says J. D. Sandoval, "is the biggest problem affecting the staff's ability to work on projects. Politicians are not trained in the technical phases of planning. When they look at a project they may have their own concepts that might differ from those of the planning department. Politicians look at political aspects of a project, whereas planners are concerned with codes and ordinances."

This difference of perspective can have adverse consequences, according to a captain. "Policy is not usually made by supervisors, but they are the ones who often have to deal with flip-flops in policy or implement unpopular ones. A policy is made by the chief. But when the city finds out, they may reverse the policy. That is a thorn when it happens to the supervisor and the firefighters. Money-type decisions always come from City Hall. One of these decisions was to have two men per engine versus three. By only having two, the city saved some money, but put the men in possible danger."

Dealing with Politicians

Despite misgivings about working with politicians, veteran supervisors believe that relations should be improved. Politicians and public servants should work together and not against each other.

Build a Buffer

Because responding incorrectly to the request of an elected official could ruin one's career, Fruchter says, "The main thing is to find out ahead of time what the organization's policy is on dealing with elected officials."

The simplest policy is one that prohibits elected officials from directly contacting workers. "We are kind of buffered in our situation by the city manager," says a parks and recreation manager. "We are not allowed by charter to take direction from individual council people or even from the mayor. They have to go through the city manager's office."

In some instances, formal guidelines are set up. "If any politician has a question," says another supervisor, "it has to be put in writing to the city manager. That sometimes is the way it has to be with certain politicians who would be calling every single department twelve times every day. We have set up procedures. If a question asked by a politician is going to take more than ten hours worth of staff work, then it has to go before the whole city council to see if we should look into it." That procedure keeps certain elected officials from monopolizing staff time. It is effective because the politicians are, in effect, policing each other.

Establish a Dialogue

Another way to deal with politicians is to establish better communication so that they know what government workers are doing. Says Margaret Mudd, "It would help if politicians knew what public administrators were really doing and the purpose of the agency. There is a need for personal contact between the two. Without that there isn't any understanding. It becomes a matter of knowing the people and what they are doing."

"The best way that I know of," a federal district manager says, "is to have meetings and discussions. I meet frequently with the local congressional people, with city managers, with mayors, and various cities that are in my area of responsibility. If I can keep them influenced and if I am receptive to their needs, or lend a positive ear, the communication that is established between us can lead to getting things done successfully."

A labor manager concurs, "There has to be a dialogue between all individuals in the workplace—particularly in the public sector as a whole. Whether they are councilpeople or county supervisors, or whatever they might be, it is critically important that they develop a dialogue with those individuals who are responsible for the management of the daily operations of the city, county, or state. There has to be that meaningful dialogue, minus the political rhetoric—not those things that sell newspapers or gain votes."

Keep Informed

A third strategy that might be taken by new supervisors is to be informed about public issues. If supervisors expect to be able to communicate with politicians, they must understand the politicians' concerns and relate programmatic needs to those concerns. New supervisors should read extensively in their own field and broadly to understand the historical, social, and economic context of the organization. Attending local, regional, and national seminars, workshops, and conferences of one's professional organization is another important way to gather information.

Being active in the community is yet another method for gaining perspective.

The supervisors we interviewed suggested other methods for keeping informed. "Part of the reason you go to council meetings," explains Fruchter, "is just to see where they're coming from on different issues. When you're ready to present your issue, you kind of know, 'Well, this one is very into this issue so let's make sure that this proposal has taken that into account.' You have to package things to fit the political environment. If you don't, you won't get very far. That's the thing that has taken me the longest to learn in my career, but it has probably been the most interesting."

Barbara Baker gives similar advice. "Legislation may or may not be positive for your program. Anyone can pass policy that may be an unavoidable nightmare. So keep informed of legislative changes and develop a good relationship (to give information that may be helpful, not threatening) with key legislators."

"Issues that involve public officials require a great deal of background work," adds an elementary school principal. "You must talk to influential and important people away from the public platform. Taking public input is very important."

Understand the Politician's Viewpoint

Another thing that supervisors can do to improve relations with politicians is to appreciate the politician's role in government rather than do battle with them or view them as adversaries. Hageman says:

It is important that all managers understand why politicians behave the way they do. If you come in as a manager and separate yourself from the elected official, you
start to forget why you are here. You're here because
we live in a democracy. The people vote their leaders
in and those people make policy. If you come in and
you're the expert—you're the engineer or you're the
manager—and you know everything and the politicians are just in your way, then you are forgetting that.
We lose the perspective of the elected official. We get
protected, as management, from the electorate and
from the community because the elected officials are
out there at night at a community meeting with people ranting and raving and calling them stupid and cor-
rupt because the pothole isn't fixed in the street. But
the guy who fixes the pothole doesn't hear that, he's
not called stupid—the politician is taking all that flak.

"Politicians have a different constituency to answer to than
managers," says a seasoned supervisor. "It is not that they
are wrong, they're just addressing a different group."

They may also have a different viewpoint, says a senior
manager:

Politicians come and go, but public servants are usually there for a career or a lifetime. In terms of the
decisions that are made, your public-service managerial person is concerned with long-term, lasting kinds
of relationships and long-term planning as far as your
organization is concerned. It is not to say that all politicians have a short-term kind of planning thought.

185

But they can be impacted and influenced by a constituency that may not have a handle on the interworkings and the necessities of the organization as a whole and the people who work in that organization.

Cantor also points out that political viewpoints may be different because politicians may have information that is not available to others.

Some of the supervisors we asked felt that the relationship between government workers and politicians may not be as bad as first thought. "Sometimes on the surface they appear to be hostile due to the nature of what is going on," says a veteran supervisor of ten years. "The director will present something to council that is really practical and should be done. But it is not appealing because it is going to step on someone's toes or cause problems for other constituencies. So the councilperson will get after the staff person. They don't really mean a lot of that. They are just doing it for political purposes to give a certain appearance."

"Sometimes there's a misunderstanding on both sides," says another supervisor rather philosophically. "The administrators sometimes don't understand the basis for the policies. Sometimes they do understand but don't agree." However, "when the administrator is arguing with the direction of the policy makers," says Linda Oravec, a politician turned public administrator, "it is time for that administrator to leave."

Be Preventive

One way to avoid problems with elected officials is to make sure that staff know how to handle inquiries and com-

186

plaints. "You have to make sure your people are polite," says Robert Nelson, "that they understand, they listen, and the last thing they say is, 'I hear what you said, and I will make sure my boss knows about it and gets back to you.' They should follow up by letting you know that the councilmember contacted them so that the problem is addressed. This protects the process." And it ensures that one's unit is responsive—in the sense of acknowledging that a complaint has been registered. Nothing gets elected officials madder than getting the "bureaucratic shuffle."

Try to deal with problems when they occur and not let them fester. "The main thing," says a senior supervisor, "is to keep an eye on things. You have a sense of all that is happening. If you see a problem, nip it in the bud." That is sound advice for most problems that face supervisors, but particularly important for seemingly simple problems that may become heated political topics. Once political flames are fanned, it is often too late for cooler heads to prevail.

Office Politics

The initial reaction of veteran supervisors to the question of office politics is not unlike the reaction to dealing with external politics: avoid it if you can. "Stay out of it," says an athletic director. "Don't get involved," adds another supervisor. "Avoid it at all costs," warns a transit supervisor. "It has a detrimental effect on subordinate moods and attitudes about each other. It affects productivity negatively."

However, ignoring office politics will not make it go away. "Office politics [is] aggravating," according to Barbara Baker, but the reality is that it is unavoidable. Many supervisors would agree. "Office politics will always play a role in any organization," says a postal worker supervisor. "Although it shouldn't influence decisions, it almost invariably does." The question is really one of learning to live with it. Ron Friedman, a principal planner, put it this way: "Every organization has a subculture. Understand this subculture and work with it. It's the way we do things. You don't have to agree with it, but know the ins and outs of the system." A supervising administrative analyst agrees, "Realize that politics is a natural part of the work environment. Don't try to eliminate it totally. It can work to your advantage."

If you do not get involved, you will be dragged into it anyway, advises Robert Hutchinson. "Office politics is unavoidable because those people who are heavily into politics, trying to run their own myopic agendas and getting their own nests feathered within the organization, are trying to get as much support as they can from anybody. A new person in the organization is a spring lamb to be brought into their fold."

There are a number of strategies that new supervisors can adopt to avoid being the "spring lamb."

Don't Take Sides

Inevitably, political forces within the office will put pressure on new supervisors to align themselves with a particular faction. Taking sides can be dangerous, says Charles Marshall: "You might align yourself to someone politically and make the wrong choice. When people in organizations are going for different positions within the organization, they might be in a good position for a while, but sometimes things change and the overall picture changes. Then they are no longer in favor. If you have aligned yourself improperly with someone, what you did basically was put all your eggs in the wrong basket. It can come back to bite you just as quickly as it looks like it is going to help you."

Hutchinson agrees, but adds some insight: "Sometimes you're forced to go with one crowd or another in a large organization. If you avoid it entirely, then they figure you're not part of the group." There is considerable pressure to join or be ostracized.

It may sound like a no-win situation, but several of the supervisors argue for remaining neutral—not taking any sides. "Don't take sides with a particular person, group, or issue," advises Gerald Chiles, a supervising personnel analyst. "Because if you take sides, it could burn you later—especially, if you have to work with an individual with an opposing opinion." He suggests that the best thing to do is meet with the people and try to air differences.

"My advice," says an Immigration and Naturalization Service supervisor, "is to identify yourself as a neutral resource for both sides. The key is not to get caught up in the political turf wars and the cultural and social interaction among dominant groups in the organization."

According to a Drug Enforcement Administration supervisor, more is at stake than being on the wrong side. "A supervisor should be professional and neutral in politics, because as a supervisor gravitates towards a particular person or group, the supervisor begins to lose credibility." In other words, it becomes very difficult to be a leader—one of the major functions of a supervisor.

Don't Gossip

Judging by the popularity of the many colorful tabloids at the grocery checkout stand, it seems to be human nature that we like to hear the worst about others. But gossip and rumors in the context of office politics are also statements about power and influence. Most supervisors realize they should not gossip. However, if supervisors actively listen to gossip, are they openly encouraging character assassination, are they taking sides, or are they merely seeking useful information to corroborate rumors in the grapevine?

Baker makes a good suggestion: "Before office politics get out of hand, be direct, honest, and unwilling to listen to gossip. Address gossip by telling employees to deal with it out of the workplace. Get gossip under control as soon as possible."

If the supervisor knows who is gossiping, Bobbie Shaw suggests going right to the source. "Talk to the individual you think is promoting the politics," she says, "and attempt to nip it in the bud."

"See who is involved," says yet another supervisor. "If it starts to get out of hand, investigate, and, if warranted, call people in and let them know it must be stopped." One has to be careful, however, because "if you make a big deal about it, you might lend credence to it." If it is occurring outside of the workplace, one supervisor suggests dealing with it, too. "Tell them, 'Thank you, I've listened, but I'd rather not be involved.'"

A personnel supervisor suggests a somewhat different

strategy. "If an employee is having a problem with other employees," she says, "I let them know that when they come to me to talk about it, it is extremely confidential." That is, the concern is heard in the proper arena, but the supervisor is clearly in control of what happens to the information. This approach eliminates the added pressure of office politics and heightened emotions. For this strategy to work, of course, the supervisor must have a steady track record for fairness and integrity. "Keep your nose to the grindstone," says a postmaster. "Don't spread rumors or start rumors. Be careful who you talk to and what is said."

"Diarrhea of the mouth can get you in trouble," quips a personnel specialist.

"I think it is easy [to stay out of it]," answers a recreation director for a small city. "I'm more of a listener. So you can tell me what you want to, and then I do whatever I think is important—remember some things, throw out the stuff that I think is garbage, and keep my mouth shut. People will say, 'What is your opinion?' I say, 'Well, I really haven't had a chance to stop and think about it. That's a good question. I ought to spend some time thinking about it.' Be selective in your responses to individuals."

Do Your Job

Remember what the job of a supervisor is. A public information supervisor explains, "I would advise a new supervisor to keep uppermost in his or her mind the fact that the work of the unit has to come before any other kind of consideration. Politics do enter into work situations, but they should not be allowed to overwhelm the overall objective of that particular work unit. Politics should be kept at a minimal level."

"It's important to focus on job descriptions and the responsibilities of employees," says a fire chief with over twenty years of experience, "then disregard all those other things that enter in. As a supervisor, you have to focus on what the job is and just sidestep the politics. That other stuff will finally die if you zero in on the job."

One reason for a supervisor to focus on the job is that the supervisor's own boss will be watching. "The main thing to remember is that your job is on the line," a personnel supervisor suggests. "Show your supervisors that you are not going to get involved with office politics because it is not going to help you in the long run. If you spend your time dealing with office politics and controlling other people, then you are not going to be giving the time to the job that you and your subordinates should be doing."

One's subordinates will be watching, too. "Trust that you are going to be recognized by both sides for doing a good job," says Charles Marshall, "and you will be. Develop a good reputation—showing initiative, being a hard worker [and] a go-getter, being competent in what you do, and being honest in your dealings. Try not to be a manipulator. Do the job that is spelled out for you in the rules and regulations."

Set a Good Example

Setting a good example can have a profound effect, Hutchinson argues. "If the organization has good leadership and a good esprit de corps, people are wrapped up in the or-

192

ganization and everyone is running in the same direction. When an organization does not have a good esprit de corps, people start going myopically after their own agendas to protect themselves because they no longer trust the organization to take care of their real or assumed needs. If you always make your decisions in support of the organization, you could pretty well circumvent a lot of the petty agendas and politics."

If you do get caught up in office politics, learn from it. Says Marshall, "Sometimes you can get caught up in something or get carried along in different aspects of politics and not be aware that you have been manipulated. Part of politics implies manipulation. You need to learn how to recognize manipulation. Once you recognize it, don't let yourself get caught up in it. Recognize the positive example you set. It is important for you to present yourself to your subordinates as fair, confident, honest, and trustworthy. The only way you can portray that is to be that way."

Although supervisors should be friendly with their workers, that does not necessarily mean sharing secrets or becoming personal friends. "Keep your private life to yourself," counsels David Labadie. "Keep relationships as professional as possible. Avoid personal bonding with employees or it may turn to trouble down the road."

"Do not get socially involved with the staff, except at staff functions," adds an elementary school principal. "It creates too many problems. There will always be people you like more than others, but keep it professional—good manners, not too familiar, watch jokes, etcetera. Watch yourself."

And If All Else Fails?

Veteran supervisors seem to agree that if office politics cannot be worked around, then it must be squarely faced. "A new supervisor needs to deal with problems immediately," says a postal supervisor. "If problems are not addressed, they will bite you. An action needs to be taken or the problem will grow out of proportion."

One supervisor suggests that some things cannot be changed. Therefore, "just try to stay up on the attitudes of staff and regulate the environment" as positively as you can.

However, if things are really bad, one may have to follow the last-resort advice of a community college program director. "People have different values and personalities," she says. "Therefore, managers cannot tolerate personal conflicts. If people do not get along, they will have to leave. The manager cannot let it impact the office."

To Summarize

Internal office politics and external political pressure can be vexing problems for new supervisors. What they learn quickly is that politics is an integral part of the public sector workplace that cannot be avoided. To survive requires that supervisors become adept at dealing with the repercussions of politics.

To deal with external politics requires understanding the politician's point of view and being able to distinguish between the politician's role of setting policy and the supervisor's role of implementing policy. Although the distinction can become quite blurred, supervisors can become more effective by establishing a dialogue with policy makers and community leaders and by building buffers to reduce the direct impact of political decisions.

Managing office politics also requires communication with key stakeholders in the workplace. Setting a good example and explaining the reasons behind one's decisions are ways to anticipate the consequences of internal politics. The goal, of course, is not to eliminate office politics, but to make sure everyone is playing by the same rules and the playing field is as level as possible.

Items for Reflection

1. Prepare a report that summarizes interviews with several supervisors in government agencies in your area about policies for handling inquiries and complaints by elected officials.

2. An elected official has taken a personal interest in an issue that is currently under study in your unit. The elected official has made it clear what the desired outcome should be. There is an implied threat that there will be trouble if you do not go along. Describe how this situation should be handled. How could it be prevented?

3. A worker in your unit always seems to disagree with your decisions, but never to your face. Rumors are spreading about the adequacy of your supervisory capacity. What do you do?

4. Two opposing factions in the organization want you to be on their side. Joining one side will make the other side mad at you. Failure to take a stance means that both factions will likely attack you. Describe what you would do under the circumstances.

9

Handling Public Relations

Experienced supervisors tend to view the media, both print (newspapers, magazines, and tabloids) and electronic (television and radio), with some degree of trepidation. Perhaps Daniel Del Castillo summarizes the sentiment best when he says, "The media is the best ally and the worst enemy." On the one hand, the media can play an important role by informing the public about available services such as a new health program for the elderly or by building citizen support for a needed project like water conservation during the recent drought in southern California. Yet, at the same time, the media can also be a harsh and unrelenting critic of the public sector. At times it seems as though public organizations are under a microscope with the press relentlessly probing and searching for the slightest mistake to portray public servants as inept, insensitive, and inefficient.

The job of a supervisor is made much more difficult with the knowledge that the media is always there—waiting for leaks from dissatisfied employees, watching for the latest criticism from special interest groups, and hoping for impending lawsuits that will embarrass public organizations. To some supervisors, it seems as though the next crisis is uncovered before the first is ever taken care of.

What can supervisors do to avoid having an embarrassing incident turn into headline news, a media interview look as though agencies were hiding something, or a quote out of context turned around so that the meaning and intent of one's statement portrays public servants in the worst possible way?

In this chapter we suggest that there are ways to deal with the media *before* there is a problem and, more importantly, that relations between news reporters and supervisors can be improved to the benefit of both. We begin by trying to understand the relationship between media and governmental entities.

Understanding the Media

At times, the media can be such a thorn in the side of some supervisors that there is animated discussion around the office about limiting the media's access to information, stonewalling their inquiries, and devising regulations that would stymie even the most determined investigative reporter. As tempting as these solutions may be, supervisors need to examine carefully their attitude toward the media first. Troublesome as the media may be at times, it does serve an important function in our society. Very simply put, freedom of speech and freedom of the press are vital institutions in our way of life. It is in part this diversity of opinion and open discussion of differences that has made this nation what it is today. While we may not always agree with the way the media presents the news, imagine what it would be like to live in a country where the news was so controlled that one heard only what a certain few wanted one to hear. "The free press," says Patricia Zamary, "represents democracy. The public has a right to know."

Tempting as it may be to censor the press, to withhold information, or to limit access to government documents because journalists do not always present the public sector in the best light runs counter to the Constitutional imperative guaranteeing an independent press. The First Amendment is designed to protect us against a secret government that might operate in its own interest and against its citizenry. Weighing the problems posed by an errant press against the greater danger of an uninformed public was as much a problem in colonial times as it is now. In the end, the founders of this country decided that trying to protect against an imperfect press would cause more problems than it would alleviate. In essence, a democratic society requires a free press that is able to keep public institutions "honest," so to speak. "Without the media," says a labor relations manager, "people would be relatively uninformed. It increases people's awareness and opportunity to know and be involved." That is what democracy is about: participation.

For the most part, in the opinion of Ruth Ann Hageman,

"The media is very responsible. They have a job that is absolutely essential in a democracy—to tell the truth to the public. The reporters who report on the city are excellent. They learn things very quickly, they get the facts right, they write well."

"On the other hand," she also warns, "sometimes reporters have their eye on a prize or on the opportunity to create a sensation which will sell more newspapers." Kevin Hardy agrees that the "facts" are always reported. "You also have to realize," he says, "that journalists have editors and owners who want to project and advance a certain agenda as well. They're human beings, just like the rest of us, and they've got their own interests." In a pluralistic society made up of many special interest groups, Hardy's comment is not surprising. The media has several interests at stake in what it reports.

One of those interests is the portrayal of a certain quality of life in a community. "You need to be careful," a school administrator warns. "The news is very influenced by the image of the community. They build it rather than report it." Whether the image is that of a center of commerce, a major manufacturing hub, a place for clean industries, a tourist mecca, a suburban refuge, or a quiet rural community, the print and electronic media attempt to reinforce and influence community values and standards. Whether we concur with their particular position or not, most of us would have to agree that it is an important role for the media to play.

A second interest is political in nature. "The things that seem to generate interest from the media perspective are the political things. Those are much more highly charged and much more likely to be twisted and turned to meet the political agenda," says Hardy. "If the local media doesn't like something one of the councilpersons is doing, or if they don't like the way the water utilities company responded to the mayor's water usage request—then they are going to twist that to make it work the way they want it to." While this may sound like biased reporting to some, advocating a position is part of the American process. The media need not be neutral, because viewers, readers, and listeners tend to compensate for the bias. That is, the position of the various media on political issues is usually fairly well known, and the public takes that into account when reviewing the news.

A final media interest is clearly economic. "The media only reports what sells papers," says a group supervisor for a federal agency. That may explain why incidents that reflect positively on public agencies are often not reported: good news does not sell as readily as stories about the unusual, uncommon, atypical, exceptional, and novel. It may also explain why certain incidents are sensationalized for maximum exposure. Whatever the reason, the bottom line is that unless the media makes a profit, it cannot do its other job of informing the public.

Supervisors may disapprove of these political and pecuniary interests, in the opinion of a large city personnel director, but we still should not condemn the press. A free press does not mean there has to be consensus. "They distort, exaggerate, misrepresent, and they get the story wrong," he argues. "But I have zero criticism of them for doing it. They have a job to do: reporting news as they see it. I don't like it, it makes me angry, but it's their job to do that. If I was selling newspapers, I'd do exactly what they do. I don't own a newspaper, I don't agree with what the press says, and I'm not a defender of the press, but if you don't like it then start your own or sue them. Other than that—and I've been criticized by the best of them—take your lumps or get out of the public eye." Media involvement comes with the job of supervisor. While we may not always agree with the media's methods or agenda, it has an important role to play in our society. The media is a given that we must learn to live with and work around.

What About Fairness?

In spite of what has been said, understanding the role played by the media and accepting some of its practices may be very different matters. This section deals with two concerns that illustrate the tension: the apparently negative attitude of the media toward public sector organizations and the exploitation of horror stories. Our point here is not to make excuses for the media, but to suggest that it may not be as unfair as we might believe.

Negative Attitude

Many supervisors surmise that the media has a bias against public agencies. "It is difficult for supervisors and their respective agencies to improve their images with the media," says a Drug Enforcement Administration agent, "because the media already has the agency prejudged." And usually in a negative way.

Cheryl Fruchter agrees. "If you work for a private company and you find a way to save money," she observes, "you announce it, and everyone says, 'Oh, that's great you did this.' In government, if we go in and start saving a lot of money or [being] more effective, the first thing you hear is, 'Why didn't you do it this way in the first place?' So you tend not to publicize your successes because you get negativity back for it."

While there may be some truth in what these supervisors are saying, a more careful examination of the issue is called for before making any generalizations. First of all, public organizations are engaged in many activities that are highly controversial, both in a philosophical sense like the current debate over abortion rights as personal choice versus society's responsibility, and in a practical sense when some groups in society will benefit at the expense of others as a result of government action or inaction. As a result, debate over public policy is all at once inevitable, desirable, and heated. Each interest group will make its best case for or against government action before the policy is made law and afterwards as agencies implement the mandate. If one side wins, the other side loses. If there is a compromise, both sides may feel slighted.

The point here is that the negative attitude that the press seems to have toward the public sector may be an artifact of the policy-making process, where public organizations are placed in the unenviable position of implementing programs that will be criticized by one group or another. Says Leroy Brady, "Sometimes you can't be right. For instance, if someone asks if there is racism in the city, no matter how you answer it, someone will think you are crazy."

The political atmosphere surrounding the public sector means that every decision carries political ramifications. And where there is politics, there is scrutiny of intent and purpose as well as attempts to influence. "Anything that a public organization is involved in," states a land use planner, "is going to get negative publicity—it's political. Since people's tax dollars are in it, there is a higher interest in the wrongs than in the rights."

"When it comes to things such as money and spending the taxpayers' money," adds a naval civil servant with his own example, "the media will always have an interest in things like that. If we get a new submarine that costs a billion dollars, the media will most likely cover that story and will try to dig up some dirt and controversy."

What is dug up, however, is not always what it seems. "In recent years," says a public works manager with more than twenty years of experience, "every reporter envisions himself another Woodward and Bernstein [Watergate investigative reporters]. They think that because things don't add up perfectly, the word 'cover-up' has to pop in. People just screw up sometimes. Horrible though it may sound, since bureaucracies of government are staffed by people, it has all the weaknesses of any group in society."

In some cases, the discovery is not anything new. "The media likes to make things look as if they have uncovered some big secret when it really is something that we have known about," remarks one young supervisor. As an example, a director with a quarter century of experience tells the following story:

About a month ago, in the midst of looming water rationing, a leaking sprinkler caused some problems. Because an entire building needed to have the water shut off to fix this minor problem, it was not fixed right away. However, the person who originally notified Physical Plant of the leak became impatient and called the local newspaper. The paper printed an article blasting Physical Plant for not saving water. I called the writer of the article and tactfully explained the situation while at the same time asking why they had not called me to get our side. As it turned out, the very next day [it] had been planned to correct the problem anyway!

Finally, as stated previously, bad news sells. "People expect bad news because that's all we hear about on television, radio, and in newspapers," says an employment services manager. "Negative news sells," says another supervisor in agreement. And because news gathering is a business, the bottom line is presenting whatever sells.

Horror Stories

That brings us to the question of whether the media is exploitative and only looking for stories to sensationalize the horrors of bureaucracy and government. We have to put it in perspective, says a personnel director. "Muckraking has gone on since Gutenberg invented the press. And it's only going to get better as the media gets better."

Or as a county land use planner puts it: "The media loves to find problems." But she also notes that readers, listeners, and viewers also like to hear about problems. "Of course, people like to hear about the bad stuff anyway," she continues. "It's sort of like everyone looking at the accident on the road, but nobody stopping to help the car that overheated or ran out of gas."

A number of supervisors we surveyed seemed concerned that the sensationalization of horror stories negatively affects the image of public sector organizations. For example: "Very rarely do you hear of the human interest stories," an athletics director laments, "because they are not what will sell to the people. In athletics, you hear about the people who are on academic probation or flunked out. These people are the bottom 15 percent of athletes."

According to Goodsell (1985), journalists tend to choose the bizarre and horrific cases because they know that such cases will arouse the public's interest. A favorite American story to read about is the lone citizen facing the larger, more powerful bureaucracy and putting up a good fight. To the media an elderly grandmother who is denied health care benefits because her income exceeds the eligibility limit by a few dollars is a human interest story. To the bureaucrat, it is only a matter of enforcing the rules and regulations set by others. (The irony, of course, is that should the bureaucrat make the services available to an ineligible client, there will be no end to the charges of collusion and fraud.)

In spite of that, Goodsell goes on to say that the public's perception of government bureaucracy may not be as bad as we think. In particular, those who have received government services are more inclined to think favorably about government than those who have not. This suggests that supervisors may be giving more credit to the power of the press than is warranted.

Some of the media's alleged distortion of stories may also be the result of errors rather than deliberate character assassination. "Sometimes they do get facts turned around," says a transportation planner. "When something like this happens, it usually is because of a misunderstanding rather than a deliberate distortion."

Another supervisor gives an example: "When I worked at Air Pollution Control, the media would come to our office quite a bit. When there's been a smog alert in the county, many times they fail to state that the smog alert was only in specific cities. They make it sound like it was throughout the county. So everyone is in a panic mode and we get all these phone calls."

Interpretation of what was said is an ongoing problem and mistakes are made. "Remember that it is difficult when what you say is put into writing," says a personnel analyst, "because sometimes your intentions and thoughts are not quoted exactly as you meant them. People misconstrue things very easily. When they don't know the facts, they form opinions quickly and irrationally. If you look in today's paper, you'll see several correction notices located towards the back pages that were mistakes on yesterday's front page."

Whether the horror stories are true or not, it is important that supervisors do not overreact to them. "The criticism may be useful," suggests a transportation planner, "in that it forces you to rethink how you approach an issue.

That is, it can act as a cleansing tool." As an example, consider the tale of Robin Niklas, a mail delivery supervisor for the Postal Service. On Secretaries Day, a while back, Niklas says the office secretaries received buttons as a gesture of thanks. When the press heard about it, they criticized the department for having spent money needlessly. What would be the more constructive thing for Niklas to do—complain about how government is mistreated by the media, dismiss the horror story as ill informed, or make sure that there is no negative publicity next year?

Working with the Media

So far the discussion has implied that the media controls what is said about the public sector. While there may be some validity to this assertion, it would also be fair to say that public organizations are not powerless or at the mercy of the media. There are a number of strategies that might be employed to effectively influence the media. A school administrator argues for being proactive. "You need to be aware and call the media first," she tells us. "Let them know before they find out—call a meeting. If they don't come, then you don't respond the next time they want news. With this in mind, you need to plan and to know what can happen. Get in front of it. Don't be defensive." She goes on to give an example of what she means: "A San Francisco school had government activities [and] a strong educational staff that tried to get the media to cover their computer lab and progress. But the media wouldn't. However, later there was a shooting on campus that the media wanted to cover, but the administrator of the school refused them."

While this may be an extreme example, the case does illustrate that the media needs us as much as we need the media. The supervisors we talked to had many suggestions.

Improving the Agency Image

One very common reaction to a media assault on a public agency is for that agency to close its doors and cut off communication. This "damage control" or stonewalling approach, unfortunately, often adds to the impression that the agency has something to hide and incites journalists to search even harder for more incriminating tidbits. Unfortunately, sometimes the agency does its best to respond to a news story, but by the time the public information officer gathers enough information and arranges for an official spokesperson to make an informed statement, "not only are you in trouble for what happened, you're also in trouble for covering it up," says Cheryl Fruchter. The solution is simple: "The media is quick and we just aren't," a supervisor in a large county observes. "To improve our image, information needs to be processed faster in public organizations." This is the approach that Johnson & Johnson took after the Tylenol capsule poisonings. The organization appointed a high-level spokesperson whose job it was to answer media questions quickly and accurately.

Being responsive is certainly one key to improving one's image with the media. But there are other strategies that supervisors can engage in before a news crisis strikes. One is to inform the media about agency activities in good times. "Invite them in," says a recreation services manager. "Inform the public of your successes through the media.

Let them know you are here: this is what we do, this is how we are supervised, these are our programs."

When the police department of a major U.S. city began to receive media criticism because a high percentage of criminal suspects were being shot by members of the police force, it decided to invite the media to participate in a "Hogan's Alley." Reporters trained alongside police recruits, learned about police procedures, and experienced the difficulties involved in deciding whether or not to shoot a suspect. By the end of training at the pistol range, all of the journalists reported favorably about the police department and the adverse conditions under which police work.

Public relations campaigns like this work because members of the media were invited to observe for themselves. Firsthand accounts are not only newsworthy stories, but are effective in counteracting the impression that public organizations are impenetrable fortresses that are indifferent to the average citizen. As in the police department example, Ethel Chastain suggests being open and sharing both positive and negative information with the media. If they are informed about budget constraints and other limitations on services, news reporters will have a more difficult time writing stories about clients who did not receive services because of a heartless bureaucracy. Chastain also suggests meeting regularly with news media editors—the people who decide what is or is not news.

If supervisors sincerely believe that their organizations do more good than harm, then this open-book strategy has much to say for itself. A state lottery district manager suggests "supervisors and public organizations can improve their image by providing brochures and annual reports to the public." She also recommends that "the director appear on radio and present the facts to the public."

The more personal the contact, the better. "Get to know the people," says a labor relations director. "Not only within your organization, but get to know the people receiving the services that your department is providing. When I say get to know, I don't mean you have to go to lunch with them or get out of the office seven hours out of the day. What I mean is you need some reality base for what is going on, what the concerns are, the dynamics that exist in your organization, from your employees, from your middle managers, and from your customers who are critically dependent on you to provide a service."

Citizen involvement in organizations can also be formalized through the establishment of permanent citizen advisory boards that report to management about concerns expressed by the public. A transportation planner suggests the use of public hearings as another way to learn about public concern. They also serve a secondary purpose. "We try to keep the public alert and to inform them on controversial issues," he says. The key to either approach is to give credence to these groups and individuals by responding to their recommendations.

Captain Jon Torchia goes one step further in interacting with the public. "There used to be an image of us kicking back at the station when we weren't on a call. That's not a fair image. We find it helps just to be out in the public, whether we're going to the store, checking fire hydrants, at the park, or doing drills. We make a lot of contacts with citizens and let people know we're there for them."

A single approach may be fine, but Robert Hutchinson suggests a multipronged approach:

> You make sure whenever possible that you are part of the solution to a community problem rather than part of the problem. It's very simple. At public meetings, let people know what the organization is doing. Put out a news release. It may or may not be accepted and published by the newspaper because they don't have the time. But then again, if they run out of bad news, they've got to fill their paper. Let people know that your organization has done a good job. Be a speaker at some community meetings, and let them know what your organization does. Let them feel through your presentation the pride in what you do and what the people in your organization do to help the community. That's the way to get the word out—face to face.

Develop an Ongoing Relationship

A number of supervisors mention that rather than deal with the media only when there is a crisis, it is better to develop an ongoing relationship.

Developing that relationship, of course, is not easy. "I have a very good working relationship with the media," a redevelopment supervisor remarks, "but I work very hard to keep it." Developing a good relationship with the media takes time. "I think you have to spend the time with them," reiterates a manager who works with many government organizations. "I find you're better off explaining something to them so they understand it rather than have them print something that is wrong. You get them the material so they can read it. You spend the time with them so they understand it. If they understand the issues, and the facts, they will usually write a good story. I find the worst stories are written when they're trying to do something quickly. They talk to one person on one side and not to the other person on the other side. I will tell them my side and in some cases tell them to talk to other people."

Developing an ongoing relationship with the media also means interacting with journalists in various forums. One supervisor makes sure that media representatives are always invited to city functions "so they can see the positive things the city is doing." Margaret Mudd agrees and adds that the media should be involved in activities where VIPs are present. This introduces the media to important people and gives news stories that extra "angle" that generates reader or viewer interest.

Be Open

Seasoned supervisors give many reasons for keeping on the up-and-up with news journalists. "Tell the truth and never try to cover up," says a postal service manager. "Lies tend to build up on one another and that creates an explosive problem."

"The worst thing," adds the regional director of a federal agency, "is to be caught not being up-front with the media. The media people are extremely astute and have

213

many resources. Many times they know what is going on before it goes down. If you try to evade a reporter, as minor as it may seem, it only adds to your problems."

The consequences can be dire. "You start hiding things from the media," says Kevin Hardy, "and it's like sharks to a dead fish. They get a hold of it and they're just not going to let go."

"If you screw something up," advises a personnel director, "admit it. Your image in the press doesn't matter as much as the public perspective of how good these people are—are they telling the truth? You've got to be good, because if you're not, people will see through that in a second."

To gain that trust, a U.S. Customs agent recommends always telling the truth. "I have found that the truth tends to reduce explosive situations. Be responsible for your actions and take responsibility whether you are right or wrong."

There are other reasons for being truthful. "We're a public agency," says Lee Hultgren, "so we have to be pretty open. Tell the truth. Be diplomatic." Even at that, the questions can be tricky. So Hultgren offers additional advice. "They will definitely try to get you to say things that you don't want to say," he continues. "Again, I try to be honest with them. I say, 'Look, that's not really the case. You're trying to get me to say that and I can't.' You tell them the truth in a diplomatic way. If you tell them the truth and they know it's the truth, then they respect you for it."

If you do not know the answer, then say so. Hattie Bryson recommends: "Answer only the questions you are very sure of. If you don't know the answer, be honest and say that you don't know. No one is expected to know everything."

If you promise to make changes, follow up with the media. Keep them informed. "Follow up and let them know that you have made the changes," suggests Hardy. That adds to your credibility with the media.

Be Prepared

Supervisors and their workers will be better prepared to deal with the media if they know the limits and boundaries of their jobs. The first place to begin is with agency policy. "As a new supervisor," says a personnel supervisor, "I would make sure that I have a real clear understanding about whether I could or could not make a statement to the press. As a new supervisor, it's better for you to let those whose area of expertise it is to answer the questions."

Indeed, some organizations have strict policies about who can deal with the media. "Our rules are we don't deal with any of the high political issues," says a veteran supervisor. "If somebody calls from the Board of Supervisors' Office and is making demands, our instructions are to refer them to the administrative office. Our top supervisors would be the ones who would handle it."

However, even with guidelines in place, long-time supervisors advise using caution. Issues that are supercharged by political passions create recognizable pitfalls for the most part, but some do not. Because everyone has an opinion, it is easy to be drawn into a response and regret the outcome. A personnel director tells us of his experience.

Because it is difficult to find the "perfect" police applicant, the policy of his agency is to permit the hiring of officers who may have experimented lightly with drugs at an earlier age but have no other drug history. Former and current drug addicts, of course, need not apply. Yet trying to explain this to the media in an era of zero tolerance for drug abuse is difficult. "In an interview I gave," he recounts, "I made the statement that 'I don't see why the police department would have a problem hiring people who have been involved with drugs.' Here we have the director of human resources for the Police Department saying it is okay to hire people who had been involved with drugs. This had repercussions all the way back to Washington, D.C.!"

And while areas of confidentiality tend to be clearly delineated, the question of privileged information often is not. Since controlling access to information gives one power, the astute release of information is sometimes used in organizational politics to gain the upper hand. But it must be done carefully. "Realize the repercussions of divulging information that is politically sensitive," warns a public information supervisor. "Don't be intimidated by reporters who might engage you in conversation seeking information that is known only by a select few. I have seen situations in which individuals have been severely reprimanded because they divulged politically sensitive information to the media."

Another way to be prepared to deal with the media is to train employees to represent the organization—not just to do a job, says Robert Nelson:

This is an area where I think municipal governments are the weakest. They don't realize that to the people on the street—the public—every employee is expected to know almost everything about city government. A person walks out his front door and sees a street crew out there. He goes out and talks to them. He feels that the crew represents the city and therefore they should know about what went on at the city council meeting last night, or about the tentative map that is being processed by the planning committee. As a manager, you have to train your people to be informed to know what is going on in the city—not just in their job or department. You also have to make them understand that people are going to expect them to be their contact with city hall.

Charles Marshall agrees. "It is important to train employees early about the importance of their role in public relations," he says. "That is, being a good example, being professional in the way they deal with the public. If there is any question of what you are doing, relate it to how it is benefiting the public."

The reason for having all employees engage in positive public relations is that it prevents problems from becoming news events. "Supervisors and employees deal with the public on a daily basis," says a Postal Service supervisor. "There is one rule I have for my employees when dealing with the public: treat them the way you would like to be treated. If you handle the customer in a civil way, remain calm, determine what the problem is, and try to correct it, you will have turned an angry consumer into a satisfied one."

Being prepared to deal with the media includes being able to work within their format. First, an interview with the media should be viewed as an opportunity to tell one's story rather than to answer questions. Know what you want to say and look for opportunities to present it. "Review facts," says Barbara Baker, "then respond to the media. Pull records, review, respond—tell the media of processes, facts, and conclusions." To be on the safe side, she also suggests, "Be candid, clear, and follow SOPs. Also, always let the boss know what is going on."

Second, realize that the average television news story is about ninety seconds long and contains no more than twenty seconds from any particular spokesperson. Twenty seconds only allows enough time to speak eighty-five words. "When you are talking to a reporter," Hageman tells us, "you have to be careful because they will quote you exactly. And they won't necessarily keep it in context."

Third, given the constraints, begin with your conclusion first. Be prepared, of course, to follow up with facts and reasons for your conclusion. "Newspapers have to condense stories," explains a personnel analyst. "When you do have to give them information, keep it strictly factual. Once you start telling them what you think about a situation, papers often blow minute details out of proportion."

Fourth, sometimes interviewers will ask "loaded" questions with colorful language to get a reaction. Be prepared—never repeat offensive words or phrases while mulling over the question. Once you mouth them, even in denial of having said or thought them, it is the same as if you said them. "When dealing with the media," warns a drug enforcement agent, "remember that nothing is 'off the record.'"

Fifth, if ambushed for an interview, do not do the interview unless you are prepared. Get the name of the reporter and decide about the interview at a later time. "If they catch you unawares," suggests a veteran supervisor, "tell them: 'Hey look, I can't talk to you now. Call me back in five or ten minutes.' Then sit down and write something down. Read it. Make sure everything in it is absolutely true. They will call you back if they want the story, and then you will be prepared to give them the facts."

Last, remember the Reagan–Carter presidential race. In spite of what has been said previously about sticking to the facts, a likable manner sometimes has the edge. In the electronic media in particular, body language communicates more than spoken language. Several recent presidential candidates have hired specialists to teach them how to communicate nonverbally.

To Summarize

The media is often viewed by public sector supervisors as a threat. A neutral perspective on the media would be that their watchdog function is a necessary part of our democratic society, or that they are merely doing what is required to stay in business. A much more positive attitude toward the media would be that supervisors should take a more proactive stance—communicating and building bridges rather than avoiding interaction and building barriers.

219

Because the public sector is involved in the implementation of often highly controversial policies and programs, a positive relationship with the media may prevent or at least minimize the adverse publicity and notoriety that is sure to follow. Building that relationship takes time, trust, and openness by all employees, not just those who are assigned official duties to interact with the media.

Items for Reflection

1. J. D. Sandoval, a planning director, argues that television is the worst form of media. Because of time constraints, TV programs are not able to probe issues sufficiently. Yet a veteran parks and recreation manager prefers being interviewed by television crews because "what you say is definitely what you said." What are the pros and cons of each side?

2. Consider the following statement and recommend a course of action for remedying the implied problems. "The news stories of which I have knowledge all have some degree of inaccuracy. Some have a large degree of error and some have a small degree. I think that the media doesn't take the time to verify information because they are in a hurry to put the story before the public. I don't have a very high opinion of the media."

3. What are the explicit and implicit rules in your organization about talking to the media?

4. Interview your organization's public information officer about ways to maintain good relations with the media. Compare and contrast these strategies to those found in this chapter.

10

Disciplining
Problem Employees

Generally, supervisors find that their subordinates are eager to perform their duties effectively and follow the rules and policies of the organization. When a worker's performance falls short of job standards on a regular basis, the supervisor needs to be concerned. Detecting and analyzing performance discrepancies is an important role for supervisors, but a more important function is to assist the worker in bringing that performance back to acceptable levels.

Unfortunately, when workers fall short of performance goals, an all-too-frequent response of some supervisors is to assume the worst about the intentions, motivation, and character of the "offender." Successful supervisors have a different approach that has nothing to do with blame.

For example, one supervisor states, "Most discipline problems are not intentional, they usually develop because the employee was not sure of what was expected"—a rudimentary but important distinction. If difficulties like this develop, experienced supervisors usually can remedy the situation by means that do not carry the negative connotation of discipline.

How do successful supervisors view discipline? How do they use it to their advantage? These are the questions to be answered in this chapter.

Purposes of Discipline

Before we go much further, we need to make sure that the reader understands what discipline really is. When most people think of discipline, they associate the term with punishment—in particular, harsh measures to force compliance. That is not what we mean.

One of the secrets to successful supervision is to understand that, in management terms, discipline means to teach—especially to teach self-control. Supervisors who discipline with the intent to teach will end up with workers who have internalized the organization's rules and policies. They are self-regulating. That means that supervisors can focus more time on important tasks such as strategic planning instead of wasting time constantly policing the actions of workers. It also means that supervisors do not have to worry that workers will revert to old habits, or, far worse, engage in deliberate sabotage. Ideally, a successful disciplinary process contributes to the entire team effort because the educated worker can be a role model for others rather than a burden.

In contrast, supervisors who discipline with the intent to punish soon find a resentful work force that must be continually coerced into action. More and more energy is wasted as less and less gets done. People spend time blaming each other and finding fault when time could be better spent on finding solutions.

A General Disciplinary Approach

An important idea to keep in mind is that discipline is not a supervisory technique of last resort when all else has failed. Discipline—to teach—is an ongoing process that should be reflected in the day-to-day interactions between supervisor and worker. In past chapters, we discussed a variety of managerial approaches: leadership, team building, participation, motivation, positive reinforcement, performance appraisals, work organizing, role modeling, and effective planning. Each of these is, upon careful consideration, a form of discipline. When supervisors lead, they are teaching about expectations. When supervisors encourage team building and participation, they are teaching about responsibility. And when supervisors motivate, they are reinforcing and rewarding self-discipline. Discipline should not be thought of as a separate activity, but as integral to the entire supervisory function.

One of the critical activities for successful discipline is basic to all forms of good supervision: clear expectations. Discipline intended to teach correct behavior might simply involve explaining the rules and their necessity. It is surprising how easily an apparently difficult and awkward "disciplinary problem" can be resolved by merely clarifying performance standards with an employee. This is not an activity that should be taken for granted. Misunderstandings can easily occur when communication has been rushed.

Clearly, supervisors establish expected performance and conduct standards to which employees are held. But the supervisor's job is not done until employees know what the standards are. Supervisors must clearly communicate what is expected both in terms of performance standards and conduct. In the words of one supervisor, "Try to be as clear as possible about what your expectations are and once you have done this, then it is the employee who needs to take those expectations and follow through with them."

Clarifying expectations also means that subordinates must understand what the consequences of not meeting expectations are. As one of the supervisors stated, "One of the things that I like to do is tell them right off the bat what I expect. If there is a problem, I say 'Look, here is what is going to happen. The ball is in your court now and you have to decide what you want to do.'"

Supervisors can also encourage self-discipline by having reasonable rules that directly relate to the accomplishment of unit objectives. Supervisors who overcontrol by having rule after rule after rule focus attention on ways to beat "the system" rather than on ways to make "the system" work. Supervisors who apply rules inconsistently from day to day, worker to worker, or situation to situation will likely find that the trust that is essential to the disciplinary process is missing. Similarly, supervisors who do not clearly communicate rules and expectations can expect any form of discipline to be a struggle.

Finally, supervisors should use positive reinforcement or motivational techniques rather than punishment, withholding of praise, and removal of incentives to assure the best performance and conduct of subordinates. Although it is common to talk about motivation as a separate supervisory strategy, it is, in fact, a form of positive discipline. It is a way of teaching and correcting performance in such a way that the supervisor does not have to reinforce each instance of desired behavior. Workers reward themselves because they know they are doing the right thing.

Needless to say, a small number of employees sometimes do not respond to these approaches, and disciplinary action becomes necessary.

Disciplinary Process

As one of the supervisors in our study says: "Discipline is an attempt to correct. If it doesn't work, the problem can get more serious." Successful supervisors understand that discipline works best if it is used for the purpose of correcting performance. This section suggests some guidelines in the disciplinary process that might be followed.

A prelude to discipline is the performance evaluation process already discussed in Chapter Six. A good evaluation system identifies problems as they develop. This allows supervisors to counsel with employees early on. Simple communication often is overlooked as a part of the disciplinary process, but it is extremely important and may help to avoid invoking formal disciplinary processes. When employees have problems that interfere with their performance, supervisors need to consult with them. Supervisors usually are successful in identifying the source of the problem if they are sensitive and interested in the employee. By listening and understanding the employee's problems, supervisors go a long way in helping to overcome the problems. Even though a problem may not seem very big to the supervisor, it is imperative to take it seriously because it is important to the employee.

In the process of being a sounding board, the supervisor can help the employee understand and sort through alternatives for dealing with the problem. Supervisors need to avoid being judgmental and respect the employee's need for privacy and confidentiality. In one supervisor's words, "When I do discipline, I do it behind closed doors and not in front of everyone. Employees may go away and resent that I talked to them, but they have to respect that I did not do it in front of everyone."

If performance or conduct continue to be subpar, supervisors then need to follow up with disciplinary action. Once again, the supervisor must base the action on correcting behavior that is dysfunctional to job performance or organizational effectiveness. Using discipline for punitive purposes or to humiliate someone harms more than it helps. To be effective, the supervisor needs to act promptly and on the basis of information that is as complete as possible. One of the supervisors in our study suggested: "The key when you have a discipline problem is to catch it immediately." Evaluation of the information should lead to the choice of the appropriate action.

Once a decision is made concerning the need for discipline, the supervisor should hold a discipline interview.

The purpose of the interview is for the supervisor to listen to the explanation of the employee and to explain the reason for disciplinary action. It is important to focus on the behavior in question and not on the person. Supervisors need to be serious but firm and courteous in the interview. The employee needs to be informed of available appeals processes to the disciplinary action as well. Daniel Del Castillo, a personnel management specialist, summed the process up this way:

> Disciplining employees is probably the toughest challenge as a new supervisor. However, you must meet the following criteria before any constructive or progressive discipline can be accomplished:
>
> 1. Identify the incident or issue of discipline that is affecting the work performance.
> 2. Make the employee aware that it is a problem.
> 3. After identifying it as a problem, provide suggestions or remedies and offer assistance in correcting the problem.
> 4. Identify consequences of subsequent violation.
> 5. Allow dialogue with the opportunity to work things out.

Not all performance discrepancies are necessarily amenable to discipline approaches. Substandard performance may be due to a variety of more problematic reasons.

One particular area of difficulty is conduct problems in subordinates. Typically, discipline is thought to be appropriate only if the employee is capable of improving and has had an opportunity to improve. In some instances, because of stress or possibly mental or emotional problems, an employee is not capable of improving. If trained, the supervisor may be able to identify the cause of the performance discrepancy and provide appropriate counseling to the employee regarding expected improvement. Because of lack of training and the complexity of conduct problems, it may be advisable for supervisors to refer the worker to an employee assistance program for professional help. However, if improvement is not forthcoming after a reasonable effort has been made, discipline may be necessary.

A growing area of concern and challenge to supervisors is substance abuse. Drug and alcohol misuse has become a major problem affecting employee performance. Although workers can be referred to an employee assistance program, the recidivism rate is quite high even after several attempts to detoxify. In addition, recognizing substance abuse among subordinates is not always an easy task. Sudden decreases in productivity or performance are potential signs of substance abuse problems. Repeated absences and tardiness as well as erratic behavior also may be signs.

Yet unless the supervisor actually witnesses drinking or drug taking on the job, the issue has to be handled cautiously. A supervisor who suspects substance abuse as a source of performance problems should approach the employee about the performance issue rather than the suspected substance abuse. A successful supervisor focuses attention on the performance deficiency and the need to improve. At that point, it is appropriate to inquire whether the employee would like to discuss the possible causes of the performance problem. If the employee identifies the cause as substance abuse, the supervisor is in a position to suggest possible ways to deal with it. If the employee does not identify substance abuse as the cause of the problem, the options available to the supervisor may be limited. What happens next depends on the organization's established policies. In general, supervisors cannot accuse an employee of substance abuse unless they have hard evidence of usage, such as an obvious impairment, the smell of liquor, or drug paraphernalia. Where zero tolerance has been established (particularly for jobs involving public safety), employees may be subject to random drug testing whether a performance discrepancy exists or not.

Another problem area in discipline is the question of employee rights. Contemporary discipline theorists refer quite often to the concept of employee accountability, but at the same time, it is imperative to be realistic in expectations and not violate the rights of the employee in conduct. Usually, government jurisdictions make sure their policies and rules are related to the ability of the government to do its work. Thus, discipline may be imposed for purposes such as "to promote the efficiency of the public service."

Discipline often is referred to as an adverse action, meaning that it has an adverse impact on the employee. In the process, employees also have certain due process rights. These are addressed later in this chapter.

229

Progressive Discipline

Most public sector organizations utilize what is known as progressive discipline. Progressive discipline means that the employee is given the opportunity to correct the problem behavior before any formal sanction occurs. If the behavior continues, increasingly severe sanctions are applied. Typically, there are several steps, including:

1. Informal talk or counseling
2. Oral warning
3. Written reprimand
4. Suspension
5. Demotion and reduction in salary
6. Termination

Others steps may be included or excluded from this list depending on the policy of the particular governmental jurisdiction. There also may be variation in some of the specific forms of discipline used. For example, suspension may come with or without pay and may vary in length depending on the severity of the behavior, previous disciplinary record, or overall work performance.

Step one is to informally discuss the apparent performance discrepancy. As indicated earlier, there may be a perfectly simple explanation for the substandard performance, such as unclear expectations. In some instances, workers need help with setting priorities or getting access to needed resources to finish their part of a job. A gentle reminder that respects the dignity of the worker may go a long way in both improving performance and maintaining a positive working relationship.

If step one fails to improve performance, step two is to give an oral warning. What this means is that the supervisor lets the employee know that performance must be improved to a set level or there will be specific consequences. The advantage of an oral warning is that nothing permanent is entered into the worker's personnel file. If the performance improves, all is forgiven. In many ways, an oral warning is a more formal method for expressing job expectations. Consistent with what has been said previously, of course, an oral warning is intended to teach and encourage self-discipline rather than to nag, threaten, or bully.

If an oral warning is not sufficient, step three is to issue a written reprimand. In some jurisdictions, a written warning is given before the written reprimand. A written warning is the same as the written reprimand, but a warning can be removed from the personal file if there is improvement whereas a reprimand cannot. In other words, a warning is an incentive to improve, whereas a reprimand is a statement documenting poor performance. A written warning or reprimand should state, at a minimum, the performance standard; the worker's level of performance vis-à-vis the standard; the consequences for noncompliance; and the date and time of previous warnings.

Failing the warning or reprimand, a suspension would be the next step in discipline. This usually requires the approval of upper management and must be fully justified. In the heat of battle, there is a tendency to use more force than is necessary. However, if suspension is appropriate, its purpose is to let the workers epxerience how much they miss their work, the social relationships, the status and

231

power of their position, and so on. Typically, a suspension is followed by more frequent performance reviews. For example, instead of an annual performance review, the employee may be subject to monthly or quarterly performance reviews for a specified period of time. In such a situation, it is not unusual for the employee to be put on probation and to be ineligible for promotions or pay increases. During the period of probation, the individual may be subject to automatic termination for any further infraction.

In some jurisdictions, the next form of discipline is demotion and reduction in salary. This step of progressive discipline is intended to have economic repercussions for the worker. This action may be permanent, meaning the individual will have to qualify through normal processes for promotion and salary increases, or it may be for a specified period of time, after which the employee moves back up to his or her original position if there are no further discipline problems.

Of course, some infractions are so severe that progressive discipline is not appropriate and termination must be used. Usually, the personnel policies spell out what behaviors will result in immediate termination. For example, in most cases, a major theft would usually result in automatic termination. Use of illegal drugs by police officers is likely to lead to dismissal without consideration of the intermediate steps in progressive discipline. The supervisor needs to be aware of jurisdiction policy regarding infractions, because they may vary widely.

A final thought on progressive discipline: an important rule in applying any of the above sanctions is to be consistent. As one supervisor notes, "It's your obligation to follow up with discipline, because you are going to have other subordinates watching. If they see that one employee is not being disciplined, then you are going to have more problems on your hands." The same applies to consistency of level of discipline. Lack of equity may be the basis for appeals from employees who feel they were treated more severely than someone else. At the same time, it is important to take the situation into account. The supervisor often is aware of circumstances that mitigate the discipline required. While a supervisor cannot discuss a given disciplinary action, the twin issues of fairness and equity can be addressed. The most crucial step is to clarify your expectations and discuss with your employees those circumstances that might be mitigating.

Outside Activities

Our discussion so far has focused on behavior in the organization or unit. Jurisdictions often have policies regarding off-the-job conduct of employees as well. Although these policies often are hard to enforce, some activities are prohibited based on their effects on the ability of the governmental organization to maintain the confidence of the public it serves.

The supervisor's evaluation of the appropriateness of outside activities should be based not on the nature of the activity but on its effect on the ability of the employee to perform the job. A police officer who develops a social relationship with people involved in ongoing criminal activity, for example, may be unable to perform the job of a police officer effectively in the eyes of the public. Despite what claims to the contrary are made by the officer, the effectiveness of the whole police department is brought into question in the public mind. Therefore, it is appropriate to prohibit such activity. By the same token, to avoid the appearance of impropriety, social service agencies may prohibit their social workers who moonlight in private practice from being paid to see clients actively served by the agency.

Appeals

Ordinarily, jurisdictions have processes for employees to seek review of disciplinary action. Employees commonly have a certain time frame in which they may appeal the disciplinary action to the next higher level of supervision. The request for a review is usually done in writing in order to form an audit trail that each successive level in the appeals process may review. Because due process is a critical element, timeliness of appeal and response may be as heavily weighed as the issue originally in dispute. Supervisors must understand the policy and procedures for appeal.

Other factors may affect the number and types of reviews of the disciplinary issue. For example, the appeals processes may depend on the severity of the discipline. More time and question can be given to those actions that have irreversible effects on the worker's status.

Typically, the appeals process proceeds along the organization's hierarchy to the highest administrative officer. However, procedures may also include an appeals board or committee. Especially for suspensions and terminations, an advisory board made up of citizens of the jurisdiction may have authority to make recommendations to the chief administrative officer or, in some cases, an independent board or civil service commission may actually make the decision. Localities differ widely on the question of whether an appellant may have representation through a personal attorney, union representative, or friend.

Needless to say, supervisors sometimes have a negative reaction to the appeals process—as though the supervisor's decisions are under unusual scrutiny by persons who do not know the actual circumstances. Yet, our nation was founded on the notion of due process. An appeal is the worker's day in court. If the supervisor has the facts together, there should be little problem. If the supervisor's decision was based on prejudice or unfairness, then this is the forum in which to bring it out.

Resistance to Imposing Discipline

If done correctly, discipline is, as stated earlier, a learning experience that has many positive results for worker and supervisor. Positive results include corrected behavior and enhanced productivity. Morale of other employees also is likely to improve if dysfunctional activity is corrected. Still, many supervisors are hesitant to discipline.

For some supervisors, stress is the reason for not taking disciplinary action. Obviously, employees who need discipline are not likely to take it cheerfully. If they have not responded to positive attempts to correct behavior, the sanctions imposed through formal disciplinary procedures are likely to produce further anxiety and hostility.

Supervisors who are employee-oriented in their supervisory practices may not want to jeopardize their good relationships with subordinates. Discipline may interfere with those positive relationships.

Supervisors who need to be liked may also resist using discipline. Few workers seem to express a positive attitude toward performance evaluation and discipline, whether it leads to a positive or negative action.

A supervisor who disciplines a worker runs the risk of the worker calling into question the supervisor's performance—"hanging the dirty laundry outside," so to speak.

Discipline can be time-consuming as well. The time put into initiating and following through on disciplinary action can be considerable. If the employee appeals the action, the supervisor will have to invest much more time. Supervisors often conclude that it is better to put up with the problem than to lose the time involved in taking action.

It often is tempting to ignore problems and avoid discipline. The ultimate result of such avoidance, however, is a dysfunctional organization with increasingly difficult performance problems. It is important to understand that discipline is a necessary part of supervision and that effective use of discipline results in effective organizational performance.

To Summarize

Discipline becomes necessary when employees do not perform as they are required. The most effective discipline is accomplished through clear communication of expectations so that employees know what is expected. When formal discipline is necessary, several steps are important:

1. Identification of the problem
2. Making employee aware of the problem
3. Suggestions for resolving the problem
4. Identification of consequences if problem is not corrected
5. Communication to work things out.

Should sanctions be necessary, it is important to use progressive discipline, thus allowing the employee to correct problems before severe action is taken. Disciplinary actions normally progress from informal counseling to termination, with several steps in between. Only if behavior is not corrected does discipline progress from one step to another.

Once discipline is imposed, employees should have the right to appeal to a higher authority. Appeal rights may vary according to the severity of the disciplinary sanction.

Items for Reflection

1. Assume that you are the supervisor of Janet Jones, who is the receptionist in your office. She has the primary responsibility of handling incoming telephone calls and greeting members of the public who come into the office. She directs visitors to the appropriate individual for service. Everyone likes Janet, as she is very personable and helpful to everyone. One issue has begun to upset her co-workers, however, she consistently comes in twenty to thirty minutes late. As a result, others in the office have to take and direct incoming calls and visitors to the office. It has gotten to the point

where other members of the staff are making comments to you about it.

What action should you take? What information would you be likely to want? On the surface, do you see any alternatives you might suggest to Janet, depending on the information you obtain?

2. You are a member of the personnel appeals board for your city. Identify the major concerns you would have involving any appeal that is likely to come before you. In addition to the facts of the specific case coming before you, what information are you likely to need before rendering a recommendation or decision?

3. In groups, discuss several kinds of problem workers. Role-play the progressive discipline process.

4. Describe the circumstances under which termination would be the first choice of discipline.

11

Facing
Ethical Issues

When most of us think of ethics, a not-too-uncommon reaction is to brush the topic aside as either too philosophical to have much application to the workplace or too complex for the average supervisor to comprehend. Yet many of the day-to-day activities that we engage in do involve ethics. The problem is that we do not perceive these activities as matters of ethics.

Although most of us would not deliberately lie (as Oliver North did to Congress about the Iran-Contra controversy), how many of us regularly, and without much thought, violate company policy by making personal telephone calls on the agency phone during work hours, by making a few personal copies on the office photocopy machine, by taking a few minutes extra at break time, or by leaving work a little early every now and then? It is easy to see the error in revealing insider information in the Reagan-Bush Housing and Urban Development (HUD) scandals, but are we as quick to find ourselves at fault when we tell friends about job opportunities that have yet to be posted? We do not condone the procurement scandals that seem to plague the Department of Defense, so why do we feel justified in padding the expense account a bit to make up for expenses that were not covered? We chuckle at the thought of Fawn Hall, Oliver North's secretary, hiding stolen documents under her clothes, but we do not seem to give much thought to taking pencils, paper, paper clips, and staplers home for personal use. In fact, we have several ready rationalizations for our actions: everyone is doing it, the items are not worth much, it is compensation for the time and personal resources we voluntarily contribute, and so on.

These are all matters of ethics for the individual supervisor. They are crucial questions that force us to reexamine personal standards for honesty, fairness, promise keeping, and integrity. At the same time, ethics is more than a personal situation involving choices and preferences. Like other forms of decision making, how a supervisor responds to questions of ethics communicates standards of conduct for subordinates. When a promise is not kept, when supervisors act inconsistently, and when ethics are compromised, a clear message is being sent.

As leaders and role models, supervisors must be very careful because they set the tone for the workplace. According to Peters (1987), supervisors cannot expect high quality and increased productivity from a low-integrity organization. Workers will not develop a passion for their work if they do not trust their supervisors or if they feel they are being treated unfairly or disrespectfully.

What Is Ethical?

Ethics involves decisions about right and wrong ways to act. Although this may sound like ordinary problem solving, ethical decision making is a somewhat different process. Ethical decision making may follow the general outline of the problem-solving model that was discussed in Chapter Three, but it differs in several respects. Rather than facts, ethical decision making deals with values and value judgments. This makes defining the problem very difficult because the apparent problem depends on what values are held. Analyzing alternatives can quickly become a matter of sorting out what is important for personal needs, what obligations to friends and co-workers one is bound to keep, what duties one must fulfill for the organization, and what responsibilities one owes to society as a whole. Needless to say, the contracts, pledges, and commitments are often contradictory and difficult to prioritize. The resulting conclusion also differs from those in regular problem solving. It is ideally based on a consistent set of universal principles—rules for interpersonal conduct that we would want others to abide by also. In reality, of course, not only are there a multitude of exceptions to rules, but there are also competing rules.

As several of the supervisors we asked point out, some of these rules are reinforced by organizational rules and policies. "Our actions are governed by rules, regulations, ordinances, and policies of the city," says Ron Friedman. "These are ethics. You can't make independent decisions that fly in the face of what the rules and regulations are."

While rule following is important, ethics cannot be defined alone by what we are told to do. One need only remember the "I-was-only-following-orders" defense used at the Nuremberg Nazi war crimes trial after World War II to realize that we all must take personal responsibility for our actions whether we are acting in a professional or a personal capacity. A postal service manager agrees: "Ethics is really important because we have to self-manage ourselves with self-control. There is so much available to steal and walk out the door with that the matter of ethics comes into play." Ethics involves maintaining an internal standard of right and wrong in spite of circumstances that might tempt one to stray.

According to Bennis (1989), the most important virtues for a supervisor to possess are integrity (standards of moral and intellectual honesty), dedication (an intense and abiding commitment; an absolute fidelity to someone or something), magnanimity (nobility of mind and heart; generosity in forgiving; being above revenge), openness (tolerance for ambiguity; rejection of prejudices, stereotypes, and biases).

In its simplest form, ethics means being able to look at yourself in the mirror. "When it comes down to it," says Robert Hutchinson, "if people can wake up in the morning and say, 'I'm going to do a good job today,' and at the end of the day sit down and say, 'Self, I really helped some people today—I really had a good day today,' then they can resist the temptation to become unethical."

242

The standards for public servants are quite high, according to seasoned supervisors. "Public institutions with which I'm most familiar," says an assistant executive director, "have higher standards of ethics than do private corporations. It's up to every employee, from entry-level to supervisor, to uphold those ethical standards. Because public agendas serve the public, it's very important."

To illustrate the point: "When I'm faced with these problems," says Police Sergeant Gregory Cantor, "I have a choice as to what to do with them. I would never lie, steal, or cheat for another officer, nor would I expect another to do so. The old double standard expected police officers to stand up for each other. Those days are going away fast. We are under scrutiny. So our personal values are important when we make decisions. You are never wrong if you are truthful and honest."

The Opportunity Is Always There

One way for supervisors to deal with ethics problems is to be able to recognize the situations where they might have difficulty distinguishing between right and wrong. In this section, we explore three areas that can easily turn into matters of ethics.

We warn the reader that there are no definitive answers for the questions raised. In fact, as often happens with matters of ethics, more questions may be raised than one begins with. This does not necessarily mean that there are no answers, but it does suggest that there are many tough choices to be made. In any case, the intent here is not so much to provide solutions (which usually depend on the circumstances), but to draw attention to the possibility for trouble and to begin to think from an ethics perspective.

Stealing

We are all familiar with the admonition contained within the Ten Commandments—"thou shalt not steal." But what if no one knew that something was being stolen? Or if it appeared as though the victim was not harmed in any way? Those are some of the potential problems Barbara Baker has. Her workers enter the unoccupied homes of people who are either declared incompetent by the court or who have died leaving no known relatives. The workers inventory the contents and place possessions in storage for safekeeping or for later sale at public auction. "Employees have access to money and things of value," she explains. "Although one has some control, one has no absolute way of monitoring activities. For example, two workers are in a house with an appraiser. There are objects worth a half million dollars. The ethical question arises: is the employee going to report all the objects or steal one? The opportunity is always there for stealing."

In this case, traditional supervisory tactics may fall short. Even the most carefully drafted rules and regulations will not prevent losses from occurring, because the opportunities are, as Baker states, too great. Sending two workers to every home—one to watch the other—might not work if there is collusion. Harshly punishing the ones who are caught stealing may be somewhat of a deterrent, but it is also time-consuming and can only take place after the theft has occurred. Setting up a sting operation periodically to check the honesty of workers would have a chilling effect and would likely lower morale by sending the message that management does not trust workers. That tactic might also create an atmosphere in which workers deliberately attempt to cheat the system to demonstrate their defiance of what they perceive as Orwellian.

Although not foolproof, careful screening of job applicants is an important first step. Successful supervision, however, is probably an even better answer. "If people are involved in a healthy organization," suggests Hutchinson, "they are convinced that their personal, economic, and professional needs are being met." Therefore, they are not tempted.

But there are some forms of stealing that we sometimes do not think of as stealing. Is it stealing if the item taken is of inconsequential value? Is it stealing if one is merely getting something back that was owed? An athletics coach tells us about employees who steal from employers:

> Something that happens with regularity in every organization is getting paid for not working. An example would be employees who leave two hours early saying they are sick when you know they are going to the beach. Or they come in fifteen minutes late or take excessive breaks. The small amounts of time may not seem like much, but after a week it adds up to an hour. Over a year, it equals more than a week's pay. Multiply that by all the staff and that is a lot of public money wasted.

Lest no stone be unturned, supervisors must also look carefully at their own actions. A typical instance of supervisory wrongdoing is purloining the ideas of subordinates.

245

"Often personal accomplishments are not rewarded or acknowledged to the person who actually did the work," recounts a federal drug agent. "Supervisors often take and get the credit for what their subordinates actually accomplished."

Nepotism and Favoritism

One of the hallmarks of public sector work is the notion that everyone is treated equally and fairly. Yet there are instances in which these ideals seem to be cast aside. One particular problem area is personal obligations to friends and relatives.

Nepotism, the favoring of relatives in work situations, is clearly prohibited by most organizations for obvious reasons. A frequent prohibition is that spouses may not supervise their mates. But what if the two work together in the same department and neither supervises the other? "Ethical issues come up all the time," says a labor relations supervisor. "People who are members of the same family may, in fact, be employed in the same department. The question comes up about what influence that might have, making it difficult for everyone to be treated on the same level."

The question of nepotism and favoritism is more complex than one might suspect at first glance, especially if one considers all the possible forms of familial and interpersonal relations. For example, what if the two people are not married to each other, but are having an affair? What if the two people involved are former lovers and either find it difficult to work with each other or cater to

246

each other's needs? What if a supervisor has developed a close friendship with a subordinate? What if a supervisor likes one worker more than the others? What if the worker belongs to the same social club as the supervisor and thereby has greater personal access? The rules are not always clear. On the one hand, organizations cannot prohibit certain forms of assembly (as prescribed by the Bill of Rights); on the other, these relationships raise questions about fairness, equity, and neutrality.

Conflict of Interest

Conflict of interest is another area that should be of concern to supervisors. Personal gain at the expense of others has no place in public service. Unfortunately, most agency policies define conflict of interest only in terms of financial interest. For example, personnel are usually prohibited from participating in activities such as contract negotiations in which they might have a financial investment or from receiving gifts and favors from those who do business with their agency. Policies may prohibit the use of one's position for any personal gain.

In some cases, the rules are clear, and one's duties are, too. However, in other instances, the rules are not so clear. For example, most public servants would not pass on insider information to a friend doing business with their organization. But what if a worker merely gives a warning to be on the alert and does not pass on specific information? What if the worker does, in fact, pass on the information but justifies it by saying that the same information is being passed on to other competitors? Do the same rules apply when one tells a friend about a job opening, where the gain is not money but power and influence?

We know that taking a bribe would be considered a conflict of interest. A building inspector recounts the following tale:

> Well, in our business, we work by the building codes and we don't owe anybody anything. Our job is to serve the people as a whole. Being ethical in this business is extremely important. Some people believe paying off the building inspector is a way of life. I was approached once and told the gentleman, "I hope you're not saying what I think you're trying to say. Because you can't do anything to me that would cause me to give you anything that I would not give to any Tom, Dick, or Harry. If this conversation is pursued, we'll be down at the city attorney's office."

Gift giving, in some instances, may border on being a bribe. While gift giving is a common practice in the private sector, public servants are routinely prohibited from receiving gifts of substantial value from vendors and those seeking to do business with government. One obvious area of concern is the meaning of substantial value. Some statutes specify the dollar amount, but what if there are several gifts, each just under the specified amount? What if the gift is not of much monetary value, but of high symbolic value, such as convicted Lincoln Thrift's Charles Keating's practice of introducing legislators to former U.S. presidents?

A second area of concern is that, while exchanging gifts with external sources is readily recognized as a problem, gift giving within organizations is a common practice that is not. Remembering superiors', co-workers', subordinates', and secretaries' birthdays, anniversaries, and holidays is as much acknowledgement of their contributions to the organization as it is a means of attempting influence.

Conflict of interest can occur by knowing clients. If a worker has personal knowledge of a client, for example, it is appropriate for the worker to ask to be excused from the case. "If an employee [gets] a case where she or he knows the client," says Baker, "she or he should talk to the supervisor and be assigned to a different case." But what if the worker did not know the client in the beginning and subsequently develops a personal interest in the client? Personal interest may range from giving first priority to the needs of that client to becoming intimate, as several supervisors mentioned.

Conflict of interest may also be defined as the misuse of one's position. For many supervisors, the issue is not their own misuse of power, but someone else applying pressure. For example, if someone attempts to use political pressure to obtain a job with one's agency, one could follow a personnel specialist's advice and say, "it is nice to know that councilperson Joe Brown of District Nineteen sent you, but sorry, this is a competitive process and you must compete like everyone else. You will be evaluated and judged on your merit." However, the political reality is that failure to accommodate the wishes of those who are powerful may cost you your job, your program a much needed approval of policy, or your organization its budget. Blowing the whistle on such practices may only exacerbate the situation and ostracize the whistleblower from the organization.

Conflicts of interest are not always clearly defined. The director of a fairly new convention center recently lost his job because he invited his family to exclusive parties that he held at the convention center. His justification was that he was demonstrating the catering and culinary capabilities of the convention center to potential clients who were also guests at these parties. His board of directors disagreed.

A supervisor shares with us a very complex conflict of interest story:

> The mayor committed the city to host the U.S. Conference of Mayors. In general, public money is not spent for this conference; private money supports it. Somebody has to go out and raise the money. The logical place to look for help are the people who do business with cities. For instance, people who sell fire trucks would want their name in front of all these mayors. They say they will sponsor a reception if their name is on the napkins and program. That becomes very sticky when we're under contract and in negotiations with that company. It looks like a kickback. That means that whenever we want the private sector to participate in our programs, we cannot go to the contractors who provide services to the city. And yet, those are the contractors who would have the most interest in supporting the activities. We have ethical considerations that the private sector doesn't have at all. What is considered a kickback in the

public sector is considered a normal way of doing business in the private sector.

Organizational Loyalty

Organizational membership carries with it an implicit demand for loyalty, silence, and obedience to the organization that extends beyond the explicit contract where services are exchanged for a salary and benefits. Robin Niklas summarizes the expectation best: "Learn to keep your mouth shut, keep quiet, and act like you don't know. You're expected to give loyalty to your own upper management."

In a hierarchical structure, the efficiency of the organization does depend to a certain extent upon workers following management's orders and not raising any questions. It is this dependability that is counted on to get the job done. But what happens when the organization's demands are in conflict with the workers' needs? According to Hirschman (1970), supervisors have the choice of either quitting (exit), voicing their differences in an effort to effect change, or remaining silent (loyalty). The supervisors we interviewed had slightly different responses, which can be categorized into three areas: cover yourself, quit, and it all depends.

Cover Yourself

What happens when the organization asks the workers to do something that the worker considers to be illegal or immoral? One choice is for the worker to refuse—with some assurance that the truth will eventually be heard during a subsequent investigation. But what if the request is not illegal or immoral, but a matter of preference? For example, according to Margaret Mudd, "A probation officer can make recommendations to the court and be told by the supervisor that the recommendations aren't the department's recommendations. Therefore, the worker has to make whatever recommendations the supervisor says."

There are several issues at play. Disobeying the order could be interpreted as insubordination and could cost the worker his or her job. On the other hand, following orders that conflict with deeply held convictions can cause loss of productivity due to internal stress, anxiety, and many sleepless nights. Finally, following an order that conflicts with the best interests of the community may raise soul-searching questions about one's purpose in life. "If what the organization is trying to accomplish is wrong," says Kevin Hardy, "then you have to decide whether you're going to participate in it and become part of it or whether you're going to take a look and try to make a change from the inside. Big organizations have a tendency to do things that are sometimes not justified—and for some people, that can have an adverse impact."

Tim Vasquez, chief of the environmental analysis branch of the California Department of Transportation, tells of his experiences when he was asked to rewrite a report:

A social ecologist was hired to determine if a ten-year-old environmental impact report involving the effects of a freeway through a neighborhood was still accurate or if things had changed. The social ecologist's professional opinion was that things had changed and we needed a new environmental document. This, of course, meant more money and much more time. My boss told me to rewrite the conclusion and change some numbers without doing another study. I resolved my problem by telling my boss that it was not fair to tell me to do that. Basically, I wasn't qualified as an expert to rewrite the report, but I could find another expert opinion. He resolved the problem by having me removed from managing the document. The entire situation was resolved when management decided we did need a new document.

Another supervisor tells of a similar situation. "When I was a worker at the district office, I . . . was told to give someone some supplies for personal use. This was, of course, against the rules. It was really hard for me, but I had to be firm and to explain that these supplies were requisitioned by public money and were not meant for other use. I prevailed. Now as a supervisor, I must be very firm and emphasize the importance of not taking home government property for personal use—even with my friends. If they were really my friends, they would understand my position."

Finding an alternative solution and reasoning with facts, as the preceding examples show, are two ways to deal with the problem if the person giving the orders is fairly reasonable. A third supervisor tells how she would handle the situation if she were not sure about the integrity of the order giver:

If I respected management and I believed what they [believed] was correct, then I would do it. That's just the way I think we're all kind of raised, more or less.

253

If I didn't believe it, I would voice my opinion by saying, "I don't believe in what you're asking of me, because I don't think it's right, but the thing is, you are the supervisor and I will do the job." To cover myself, I'd confirm the conversation with a letter to let them know by saying, "Just to confirm our discussion and our project that you have asked of me, I don't agree on certain issues, but because you are my supervisor, I will proceed to do your project under your conditions."

Quit

For others, absolving themselves of responsibility is not so easy. "I believe," says a public works manager, "your boss has the right to say 'I hear what you're saying—you don't think it's right, but we still have to do it this way.' If that's what he wants, then he'll have to take the responsibility for it. I have gone along with things that I didn't agree with. But I would never sign anything that said I agreed to doing it that way. I've come close to that situation. If it really gets down to ethics, you have to ask, 'Can I live with it, or am I going to quit?' I would probably quit."

Many other supervisors agree. "I don't feel like I have to compromise my values in life," a recreation manager declares. "If I had to do something I really did not feel comfortable with, I probably wouldn't work for that organization." "Each individual has his or her own set of values," says William McGuigan. "Each individual must make up his or her mind about when important values are compromised too much. Each person must have the intestinal fortitude to be able to leave when it gets to be too much."

Quitting may depend somewhat on the circumstances, according to Cheryl Fruchter. "I've been in situations in the past where I was asked to compromise myself and I quit the job," she explains. "I just didn't feel comfortable. At the time, I was fortunate, I didn't have children and I could afford to do that. But very often you're not in a position where you can afford to do that."

A postal supervisor adds some further advice. "You need to determine whether the present pursuit of this goal is a short-term hazard to your values," he suggests, "or whether it will have serious long-term consequences. You must weigh the positive and negative effects to see if it is in your best interest to abandon those goals, or achieve [them]."

It All Depends

A third category of response to the issue of organizational loyalty is based partly on compromise and the circumstances involved. Kevin Hardy's comments represent this viewpoint: "You have to give up a certain amount of yourself just to be a member of society. You have to act in a certain way. It's important that we recognize that we've already given a lot just to get where we are and whatever diversity is left after that is something that you have to nurture and keep going. Yet, while you have to allow your personal values to show forth in your work, you also have to be willing to amend those values if you're not congruent with what the organization is trying to accomplish."

One supervisor gives the following example:

Years ago when I was a welfare worker, I worked in
a unit that dealt with many young women who were
coming in to get a Medi-Cal card to have an abortion.
There was a woman in my unit who was very, very
strongly opposed to abortions. So when she would
go into the interview room to interview clients, if they
qualified for Medi-Cal, she would instead try to talk
them out of having an abortion. That was not our
role. Our role was to determine eligibility and to issue the card or deny it—not to talk to them about
the morality of abortion. You really can't preach
morality in a job where your role is to determine
eligibility.

Simply put by another supervisor, "You do not have the
freedom to impose your values on other people."

Because public policy involves controversial issues,
government will always find itself half-right and half-wrong
in somebody's eyes. It is not surprising, therefore, that public servants will find themselves agreeing with some policies and not with others. On the one hand, "A person
should not have to compromise or sacrifice any values,"
says the director of a physical plant facility. "However, various compromises of personal values will no doubt happen. This is an imperfect world and the needs of the organization must be kept in focus."

It depends partly on your role, says Marshall. "When
you are on duty, you don't always have the right to free
speech. Not everyone can say they are speaking on department policy. You can't say something that is going to be

detrimental to the organization. When you are on duty you must follow the chain of command. But when you are off duty, you can say anything you want."

"I think part of the thing you do give up, as a government employee," says Fruchter, "is your freedom of choice as far as some policy decisions go. If council says something, then even if you disagree, you follow the policy or the law."

Another way to look at it is as a team player. "You are going to have to do some things you don't believe in," explains the director of a large human resources department. "I'm not talking about illegalities or cheating. If you are a part of the team, they [management] have to understand your point of view, but once they understand it, the person in charge may make a decision you totally diagree with and you have to go along. Maybe they know something that you don't, but you have to respect their judgment."

In the Public Interest

One of the principles that underlies work in the public sector is making decisions with the public's interest in mind. We are stewards of a public trust. As good as that sounds, being a steward can be difficult because there are many ways to define the public interest.

Here is a sampling of responses to the question: what is the public interest? According to Jon Torchia, "It means acting on policies which are made with the public's interest in mind."

"It's what is for the good of the constituency," says a labor relations specialist. "It is an extension of what is good and right for people as human beings."

But what is "good and right"? A Navy civil servant put it in terms of doing no harm. "Acting in the interest of the public means you do things that will not harm or jeopardize the welfare of the people."

In contrast, a recreation services supervisor interpreted it in terms of dollars and cents. "We are a public agency," she says. "We are here to give the best service for their tax dollars. To me, their best interest means wholesome, quality, good recreational programs and facilities."

A Drug Enforcement Administration group supervisor defines the public interest by what it is not. "The public interest is what public administrators should consider over personal or private interest needs," she says.

Hutchinson agrees. "If public administrators aren't acting in the public interest, they should quit. If they are pursuing their own personal, elevated need for power, for economics, for position and authority, and they color their decisions in order to gain their own personal fiefdom, they are then moving out of the realm of the 'public good.' And they should take themselves out of that responsibility."

In a way, all of the responses are correct. "The public interest is an abstract concept that is subject to personal interpretation," says Daniel Del Castillo. "The public interest will be defined by different agencies in various ways, but the central thought of the public interest is to achieve a balance between political responsiveness, administrative efficiency, and social equity."

That is a tall order, and acting in the public interest is not an easy process. "Many times you get a choice," a personnel director quips. "Which is better for yourself, less painful, and easier? I think acting in the public interest is doing those things which are painful. You'd rather shut up and hide, but you do it anyway."

Who Should Decide

One of the ongoing debates in the public sector is over who should decide what is in the public's interest. Some argue that public policy decisions should be made by politicians, since they are directly responsible to their constituents. "Council establishes what the priorities are to be," says a district recreation manager. "If there are certain activities to be done or not done, it is really up to the council to decide that. They tell the city manager what they want done and then it is the city manager's job to figure out how to do it."

Others argue, however, that public servants should have a say in determining the public interest because they have the expert knowledge and because they do not represent any particular special interest group. "Most engineers have a certain concept from their training, as do planners, as to the best way to go," says a public works manager. "They interpret that to be in the public interest."

There are arguments, of course, against both approaches. Regarding politicians making policy, a land use planner rebuts: "Special interest groups are very political and carry a lot of weight. But it is not always in the public interest." Regarding public servants' input, a federal supervisor responds: "The problem with public administrators is that they use the public interest as an excuse for every decision they make when it really could be for personal gain."

Needless to say, there is probably a little bit of truth in each side's contention. Veteran supervisors deal with this issue in a variety of ways. "Sometimes you are going to work on things that you think aren't really the best way or that you don't agree with," says Fruchter. "But I think you express your beliefs when you vote, not when you are implementing policies. I think you have to make that distinction."

J. D. Sandoval says, "Don't base your recommendations on special interest groups. Give your best professional opinion and let the city council deal with it from that point."

Working together is probably the best solution, says a long-range planner. "As the professionals who have the training, we have to come together with the politicians to define what the public interest is." Hageman agrees: "People cannot govern themselves without information, and the government is a tremendous depository of information. People need a balanced view of government."

Paternalism

As mentioned previously, one of the dangers for public servants acting in the public interest is that they may confuse their own interests with those they purport to represent. In some cases, paternalism is justified—such as parents acting in the interests of children who are too young to make decisions for themselves. In other instances, however, the subject of the paternalistic act is perfectly capable of making decisions for him- or herself. In a society that was founded on individual freedom, paternalism, even for the best of reasons, can be problematic.

Making life decisions for individuals in the public guardian role is one of the extreme cases that could lead to paternalism. Barbara Baker asks: "How does one balance one's beliefs—religious, et cetera—with those of the client? What happens when there is a conflict? Situations are sticky because there are no black and white rules. One is forced to make a choice, and the consequences are significant." Sometimes the public guardians she supervises are the only ones left to decide if extraordinary life-support efforts should be continued or ended. "Personal values, such as caring, quality of life, and respect, play a role in deciding if the life system will be pulled even though one may not believe in those methods at all."

She gives another example of paternalism versus client autonomy:

One of the county's clients is wheelchair bound. She is placed at home and lives in a substandard house. She is cared for by a daughter, and one other daughter lives in the same house. There is violence and substance abuse in the family history. She speaks only Spanish and listens to music. One would think it best for her to be in a skilled nursing facility. But for the client, this is the best environment, because she is happy and her care is good. If one moves her to the nursing facility, her life expectancy is reduced. At the facility, she would have no privacy—so she would not see soap operas in Spanish and not hear her music, which would impede her happiness. So the best decision is to keep her at home where she is happy—

even though the decision would come under the scrutiny of other agencies.

One way to avoid paternalism is to remember that clients (or subordinates) can make intelligent choices for themselves. "Make sure you listen to them," says a U.S. postmaster. "Listen to their complaints, share their concerns, act on them, and give them a reasonable answer. We get into trouble when we don't listen to people and get back with them. Be able to reply to people whether it is good or bad news."

There is also a proactive approach to listening. "We receive letters," a recreation services manager explains. "We do surveys. Just recently we did a big survey of all the teens around here. What do they want to do, what's going on, and what's not available? From that, we are proposing a teen program." In another city, a fire department supervisor says, "There is a task force citywide for customer service." In some localities, the input process is formal and regular. "We have that with the community planning groups and residents," says a land use planning supervisor.

Three Approaches

So far, we have tried to help the budding supervisor recognize that there are ethical issues that need to be dealt with in the workplace. These issues are not always easy to identify, but once they have been, it is time to take action. What is discussed in the remainder of this chapter are three possible approaches that might serve as a foundation for one's decisions. Again, depending on the circumstances, a given approach may be more appropriate than another.

Political

A political approach would focus on preserving the methods by which conflict is resolved, that is, following rules and procedures and not upsetting the balance between competing institutions, special interest groups, and so on. The goal of this approach is not homogeneity of thinking— in fact, diversity of opinion is allowed and encouraged— but peace at almost any cost. The underlying assumption of the political approach to ethical decision making is that conflict between competing groups might become uncontrollable and be so disruptive as to destroy any chance to reach a negotiated settlement. To have any semblance of peace there must be an explicit agreement on some process for negotiation. When parties disagree on most everything else, the process for negotiation is very important. The Middle East peace talks among the Arab nations, Israel, and the Palestinians, for example, hinge very heavily on no one side attempting to alter the negotiation process. They may disagree on the terms and conditions of peace, but they cannot disagree on the method for negotiation.

The public interest, in this way of thinking, becomes more a matter of preserving the means to dialogue than achieving specific ends. Thus, if a homeless person applies for welfare but has no residential address, this approach would most likely find the client ineligible for services. The reason would be that clients receive services for which they qualify, and one cannot make exceptions to the rules. Making exceptions to the rules would obviously alter the status quo and make additional demands on the welfare system. To maintain the balance of power, a homeless person with a complaint would have to follow the proper procedures for disagreeing with the rules. These mechanisms are also available to others—filing for an administrative review, influencing legislators to change the laws, and so on.

This approach is also played out in other ways. A planner tells the story of how special interest groups utilize this approach:

> You moderate the interest groups by getting them together—by involving them with other people. We do that frequently. A typical committee will have on it the Sierra Club, the construction industry, the League of Women Voters, et cetera. The Sierra Club will say one thing and the construction industry will say something else. And sometimes they agree. Usually we find some consensus. In one instance we passed a half-cent sales tax in 1987 for transportation. We had to reach consensus on what we were going to build with the new tax. We never did get the Sierra Club's support for this. However, they didn't oppose it. That was the best we thought we could do.

> The Sierra Club knew that the taxes would eventually encourage more growth and incursions into undeveloped areas. They also knew that they could carry their case to the media and embarrass the committee. However, to do so would have jeopardized the negotiation process and possibly would have been seen as the first shot in a bloody war. By preserving the peace, they hoped their silence would buy a concession on increasing urban reserves of undeveloped land.

While a political approach may preserve the foundations of this and other alliances, it can be criticized for being more about process than people. Exchanging one favor for another and concentrating on the means instead of the ends can result in an incoherent policy and many pork barrel deals—as happens in Congress regularly.

Utilitarian

Another approach to take is utilitarian: the greatest good for the greatest number. It is a frequently used principle in the public sector. "The public interest is supposed to mean helping the most and hurting the fewest," says a planning director.

"The factors that you weigh and consider," says an administrator for a transportation district, "are taking a look at the majority, at the big picture, and at the goal of the organization." Individual cases are usually not counted.

In the case of the homeless person previously mentioned, denying services can easily be justified by this approach. Because there are only so many resources that can be allocated, it is inevitable that certain groups of people will not be served. Thus, intact families that are recently homeless are given preference over dysfunctional families and they, in turn, are given preference over single men. If these policies lead to greater good than harm, then they are good policies according to this way of thinking. If these policies have the opposite effect, then they are not good policies.

One of the criticisms of utilitarianism is that it can be used to justify injustices or to harm those not in the majority. For example, utilitarianism could be used as an argument for enslavement of a few so that the majority would be better off.

Doing What Is Right

A more difficult standard is to do what is right. This approach suggests that the principles underlying one's actions are more important than the consequences. Thus, in our example of the homeless person, if the underlying value is the positive treatment of all God's creatures, then the eligibility worker would make sure that the client received needed services—whether through this agency, another agency, or the worker's own pocketbook.

In *The Power of Ethical Management* (1988) Blanchard and Peale argue that we should ask ourselves three questions when deciding what is right: Is it legal? Is it balanced (does it promote a win-win situation)? And how will it make me feel about myself? The last question is probably the most telling. Barbara Baker says it is that "little voice" inside each of us. Robert Nelson puts it another way: "My dad used to say to me over and over: 'If you can look at yourself in the mirror in the morning, that is the test.' Every time you make a major decision, ask yourself, 'Would I like to see the results of my decision printed in four-inch letters across the front page of the newspaper tomorrow?' When dealing with matters of ethics, use basic principles of your own and ask yourself if you are able to live with your decision."

Doing the right thing means not basing a decision on what is most popular or on what will increase one's survivability in an organization. As one school principal put it, make decisions for the right reasons. "Don't do things right," she says. "Do the right thing."

266

To Summarize

Questions of ethics surround the new supervisor in virtually every aspect of the job. We have attempted to highlight some of the ethical issues that new supervisors should be aware of so they can be prepared to deal with them. For the most part, it may appear as though we ended up asking more questions than providing answers. Indeed, that was the intent—both to suggest questions that would provide a framework for examining ethical issues and to urge new supervisors to ask more questions. Whether one chooses to take a political, utilitarian, or doing-what-is-right approach to solve ethical problems, the road begins by making inquiries of stakeholders (especially one's workers) and gathering information.

While ethics seems like a tangential issue to successful supervision, it is in fact at the very heart of it. In two separate surveys of fifteen hundred and twenty-six hundred managers, Kouzes and Posner (1987) found that the quality that makes a supervisor a real leader is honesty. Workers want a leader who is truthful, who can be trusted. Workers will willingly follow leaders who have character and who are dedicated to their convictions, because these create the consistency in behavior that we know as integrity.

Items for Reflection

1. Baker argues, "Just because a client chooses to live a life-style one finds unacceptable, we do not have the right to intervene in the life of an old man with a million dollars in the bank and living in a school bus." Explore your value system. Prioritize

267

your values. Is this a case of paternalism? Justify your stance.

2. You are working in a school system where sex education is a heated topic. The nurse and the counselors say that students will ask them about birth control, AIDS, and sexually transmitted diseases only if their inquiries are not communicated to their parents. The parents have generated quite a stir with the media and are pressuring the school board to disclose all conversations about sex. They argue that the school is encouraging sexual promiscuity. Develop a position paper for the school board that explains the important issues, principles, and values involved: freedom of speech, confidentiality, sexuality in teenagers, parental responsibility, the role of education, and so on.

3. You have been taking classes at a local university. The instructor has invited the entire class to participate in the first ever productivity conference that will train key leaders in the concept. You are interested in the topic and submit the necessary forms at your place of work to attend the conference. However, your request for leave is denied because your superiors do not want the conference to be a success. What do you do? Describe the steps you went through to reach your decision. Describe the conflicting values. List the underlying principles involved and explain why they are important.

4. Although legislative bodies may set the overall poli-

cies, supervisors have the opportunity to bend and reinterpret rules. Using an example from your own workplace, examine under what circumstances it would be appropriate for your professional judgment to supersede the intent or the letter of the law. Categorize these responses as political, utilitarian, or doing what is right.

5. It was suggested in the chapter that one way to deal with stealing, nepotism or favoritism, and conflict of interest was to use good supervisory techniques and to hire the best people possible. Describe possible supervisory techniques that would encourage an ethical work environment.

References

Adams, J. S. "Injustice in Social Exchange." In L. Berkowitz (ed.), *Advances in Experimental Social Psychology*, Vol. 2. San Diego: Academic Press, 1965.

Barnard, C. I. *The Functions of the Executive.* (30th anniversary ed.) Cambridge, Mass.: Harvard University Press, 1968. (Originally published 1938.)

Bennis, W. *Why Leaders Can't Lead: The Unconscious Conspiracy Continues.* San Francisco: Jossey-Bass, 1989.

Blanchard, K., and Peale, N. V. *The Power of Ethical Management.* New York: Fawcett Crest, 1988.

Bryson, J. M., and Roering, W. D. "Applying Private Sector Strategic Planning in the Public Sector." In J. M. Bryson and R. C. Eisenweiler (eds.), *Strategic Planning: Threats and Opportunities for Planners.* Chicago: Planners Press, 1988.

Cleary, C., Hanley, P., and Sopp, T. "The City of San Diego:

An Achieving Organization." *National Civic Review,* 1990, *79,* 245–253.

Dalkey, N. *Delphi.* Santa Monica, Calif.: Rand, 1967.

Delbecq, A. L., Van de Ven, A. H., and Gustafson, D. H. *Group Techniques for Program Planning: A Guide to Nominal Group and Delphi Processes.* Glenview, Ill.: Scott, Foresman, 1975.

Denhardt, R. B. *The Pursuit of Significance.* Belmont, Calif.: Wadsworth, 1993.

Etzioni, A. "Mixed-Scanning: A 'Third' Approach to Decision Making." *Public Administration Review,* 1967, *27,* 385–392.

Fiedler, F. E., and Cherers, M. M. *Leadership and Effective Management.* Glenview, Ill.: Scott Foresman, 1974.

Follett, M. P. "Creative Experience." In H. C. Metcalf and L. Urwick (eds.), *Dynamic Administration.* New York: HarperCollins, 1940.

French, J. R. P., Jr., and Raven, B. "The Bases of Social Power." In D. Cartwright and A. Zander (eds.), *Group Dynamics: Research and Theory.* (3rd ed.) New York: HarperCollins, 1968.

Gabris, G. T. "Monetary Incentives and Performance: Is There an Administratively Meaningful Connection?" In M. Holzer (ed.), *Public Productivity Handbook.* New York: Marcel Dekker, 1992.

Goodsell, C. T. *The Case for Bureaucracy: A Public Administration Polemic.* (2nd ed.) Chatham, N.J.: Chatham House, 1985.

Gulick, L., and Urwick, L. (eds.). *Papers on the Science*

of Administration. New York: Institute of Public Administration, 1937.

Guy, M. E. "Managing People." In M. Holzer (ed.), *Public Productivity Handbook.* New York: Marcel Dekker, 1992.

Halachmi, A. "Strategic Management and Productivity." In M. Holzer (ed.), *Public Productivity Handbook.* New York: Marcel Dekker, 1992.

Herzberg, F. *Work and the Nature of Man.* Cleveland: World, 1966.

Hirschman, A. O. *Exit, Voice, and Loyalty.* Cambridge, Mass.: Harvard University Press, 1970.

Janis, I. *Groupthink.* (2nd ed.) Boston: Houghton Mifflin, 1982.

Kanter, R. M. *The Change Masters.* New York: Simon & Schuster, 1983.

Kouzes, J. M., and Posner, B. Z. *The Leadership Challenge: How to Get Extraordinary Things Done in Organizations.* San Francisco: Jossey-Bass, 1987.

Lawler, E. E., III. *Motivation in Work Organizations.* Pacific Grove, Calif.: Brooks/Cole, 1973.

Lindblom, C. E. "The Science of Muddling Through." *Public Administration Review,* 1959, *19,* 79–88.

McCaffery, J. L. "Making the Most of Strategic Planning and Management." In R. E. Cleary and N. L. Henry, and Associates (eds.), *Managing Public Programs: Balancing Politics, Administration, and Public Needs.* San Francisco: Jossey-Bass, 1989.

McGregor, D. *The Human Side of Enterprise.* New York: McGraw-Hill, 1960.

Maslow, A. *Motivation and Personality.* New York: HarperCollins, 1954.

Mayo-Smith, I., and Ruther, N. L. *Achieving Improved Performance in Public Organizations: A Guide for Managers.* West Hartford, Conn.: Kumarian Press, 1986.

Mintzberg, H. *The Nature of Managerial Work.* New York: HarperCollins, 1973.

Nutt, P. C., and Backoff, R. W. *Strategic Management of Public and Third Sector Organizations: A Handbook for Leaders.* San Francisco: Jossey-Bass, 1992.

Pearson, G. *The Competitive Organization.* New York: McGraw-Hill, 1992.

Peters, T. *Thriving on Chaos: Handbook for a Management Revolution.* New York: HarperCollins, 1987.

Pflaum, A. M., and Delmont, T. J. "External Scanning: A Tool for Planners." In J. M. Bryson and R. C. Eisenweiler (eds.), *Strategic Planning: Threats and Opportunities for Planners.* Chicago: Planners Press, 1988.

Scholtes, P. R., and others. *The Team Handbook: How to Use Teams to Improve Quality.* Madison, Wis.: Joiner Associates, 1988.

Scott, W. G. *Chester I. Barnard and the Guardians of the Administrative State.* Lawrence: University Press of Kansas, 1992.

Senge, P. M. *The Fifth Discipline.* New York: Doubleday Currency, 1990a.

Senge, P. M. "The Leader's New Work." *Sloan Management Review,* 1990b (Fall), 7–23.

Simon, H. A. *Administrative Behavior: A Study of Decision-*

Making Processes in Administrative Organiza-tions. (3rd ed.) New York: Free Press, 1976.

Tannenbaum, R., and Schmidt, W. H. "How to Choose a Leadership Pattern." *Harvard Business Review,* 1958, *36* (2), 95–101.

Thompson, V. A. *Modern Organizations: A General The-ory.* New York: Knopf, 1961.

Vroom, V. H. *Work and Motivation.* New York: Wiley, 1964.

Vroom, V. H., and Yetton, P. H. *Leadership and Decision-Making.* Pittsburgh, Pa.: University of Pittsburgh Press, 1973.

White, R., and Lippitt, R. "Leader Behavior and Member Reaction in Three 'Social Climates.'" In D. Cart-wright and A. Zander (eds.), *Group Dynamics: Re-search and Theory.* (3rd ed.) New York: Harper-Collins, 1968.

Wrong, D. H. *Power: Its Forms, Bases, and Uses.* New York: HarperCollins, 1979.

Suggested Readings

Bowman, J. S. (ed.). *Ethical Frontiers in Public Management: Seeking New Strategies for Resolving Ethical Dilemmas.* San Francisco: Jossey-Bass, 1991.

Bryson, J. M. *Strategic Planning for Public and Nonprofit Organizations: A Guide to Strengthening and Sustaining Organizational Achievement.* San Francisco: Jossey-Bass, 1988.

Bryson, J. M., and Eisenweiler, R. C. (eds.). *Strategic Planning: Threats and Opportunities for Planners.* Chicago: Planners Press, 1988.

Checkoway, B. *Strategic Perspectives on Planning Practice.* Lexington, Mass.: Lexington Books, 1986.

Cooper, T. L. *The Responsible Administrator: An Approach to Ethics for the Administrative Role.* (3rd ed.) San Francisco: Jossey-Bass, 1990.

Covey, S. R. *Principle-Centered Leadership.* New York: Simon & Schuster, 1990.

Denhardt, K. G. *The Ethics of Public Service: Resolving Moral Dilemmas in Public Organizations.* New York: Greenwood Press, 1988.

Fiedler, F. E. *A Theory of Leadership Effectiveness.* Glenview, Ill.: Scott, Foresman, 1974.

George, C. S., Jr. *The History of Management Thought.* Englewood Cliffs, N.J.: Prentice-Hall, 1972.

Greiner, J. M., and others. *Productivity and Motivation: A Review of State and Local Government Productivity and Initiatives.* Washington, D.C.: Urban Institute Press, 1981.

Guy, M. E. *Ethical Decision Making in Everyday Work Situations.* New York: Quorum Books, 1990.

Hannaford, P. *Talking Back to the Media.* New York: Facts on File, 1986.

Hegarty, C. *How to Manage Your Boss.* New York: Ballantine Books, 1984.

Herzberg, F., Mausner, B., and Snyderman, B. B. *The Motivation to Work.* New York: Wiley, 1959.

Hilton, J., and Knowblauch, M. *On Television! A Survival Guide for Media Interviews.* New York: AMACOM, 1986.

Hochheiser, R. M. *How to Work for A Jerk.* New York: Vintage Books, 1987.

Josefowitz, N., and Gadon, H. *Fitting In: How to Get a Good Start in Your New Job.* Reading, Mass.: Addison-Wesley, 1988.

Karas, C. C. *How to Cope with Stress.* New York: Ballantine Books, 1987.

Katz, R. L. "Skills of an Effective Administrator." In *Business Classics: Fifteen Key Concepts for Managerial Success.* Cambridge, Mass.: Harvard Business Review, 1975.

Kennedy, M. M. *Office Warfare: Strategies for Getting Ahead in the Aggressive '80s.* New York: Fawcett Crest, 1985.

Lewis, C. W. *The Ethics Challenge in Public Service: A Problem-Solving Guide.* San Francisco: Jossey-Bass, 1991.

Nigro, L. G. (ed.). *Decision Making in the Public Sector.* New York: Marcel Dekker, 1984.

Oncken, W., Jr. *Managing Management Time.* Englewood Cliffs, N.J.: Prentice-Hall, 1984.

Pastin, M. *The Hard Problems of Management: Gaining the Ethics Edge.* San Francisco: Jossey-Bass, 1986.

Smircich, L., and Morgan, G. "Leadership: The Management of Meaning." In T. Heller, J. VanTil, and L. A. Zurcher (eds.), *Leaders and Followers: Challenges for the Future.* Greenwich, Conn.: JAI Press, 1986.

Smith, P. B., and Peterson, M. F. *Leadership, Organizations, and Culture.* Newbury Park, Calif.: Sage, 1988.

Steiss, A. W. *Strategic Management and Organizational Decision Making.* Lexington, Mass.: Lexington Books, 1985.

Tregoe, B. B., Zimmerman, J. W., Smith, R. A., and Tobia,

P. M. *Vision In Action.* New York: Simon & Schuster, 1989.

Volcker, P. *Leadership for America: Rebuilding the Public Service.* Lexington, Mass.: Lexington Books, 1990.

Ziegenfuss, J. T., Jr. *Designing Organizational Futures: A Systems Approach to Strategic Planning with Cases for Public and Non-Profit Organizations.* Springfield, Ill.: Charles Thomas, 1989.

Index

A

Acceptance: of authority, 120–121; in transition, 42–43
Accountability: and management, 120–124; and organizational goals, 122–123
Action plans, in strategic planning, 161–163
Adams, J. S., 112
Aid to Families with Dependent Children, 58–59
Appeals, on discipline, 234–235
Appreciation: by leaders, 95; showing, 23–24
Arizona, Medicaid and, 58–59
Authority, acceptance theory of, 120–121

B

Backoff, R. W., 156, 158, 164
Baker, B., 19, 42, 48, 61, 64, 67, 71, 87, 136–137, 140, 146, 184, 187, 190, 218, 244, 249, 261–262, 266, 267
Barnard, C. I., 89–90, 120, 151
Bennis, W., 242
Bernstein, C., 204
Blanchard, K., 266
Brady, L., 15, 19, 63, 180, 203
Brainstorming: for decision making, 72, 74; for vision, 157
Bribery, ethical issues of, 248–249
Bryson, H., 22, 214–215
Bryson, J. M., 153, 156
Budgeting, function of, 13–14
Bush, G., 86, 240

C

California State Lottery, and problem solving, 58
Cantor, G., 24, 70, 115, 176–177, 186, 243